Child COLLECTIVE

CONNOR BOYACK

FOREWORD BY GLENN BECK

MW01242733

Copyright © 2022 by Connor Boyack.

All rights reserved. Printed in the United States of America. No part of this book may be used or reproduced in any manner whatsoever without written permission except in the case of brief quotations embodied in critical articles or reviews.

Libertas Press
2183 W Main #A102
Lehi, UT 84043

Children of the Collective / Connor Boyack — 1st ed.

ISBN-13: 979-8-88688-005-2 (paperback)

For bulk orders, send inquiries to: info@libertas.org

PRAISE

"Fighting for freedom in the halls of Congress has made me realize this simple truth: America won't be saved by legislators, litigators, or lobbyists. Our best hope is in how we raise our children and build civil society together. Connor Boyack's compelling book explains why strong families are what will shrink the state's footprint. *Children of the Collective* is a call to action desperately needed for our day."

— **Mike Lee**, United States Senator

"Connor Boyack has hit a home run with this must-read book for all who love liberty. I'm often asked by young people what they can do to advance freedom. Now, the answer is simple: start by reading *Children of the Collective!*"

— **Ron Paul**, former Congressman and presidential candidate

"Social science and political philosophy are seamlessly melded by Connor Boyack. The most powerful conclusion of social science in the last 50 years is the predictive importance of family structure: Children from strong, intact families are apt to flourish; children from weak, fractured families are apt to struggle. Boyack demonstrates two propositions: Only a society of healthy families, which transmit the habits and dispositions necessary for individual flourishing, can be lightly governed by limited government. And unhealthy families beget tyranny."

— **George Will**, Pulitzer Prize-winning columnist

DEDICATION

To my parents—and their parents—for helping
me learn and live the importance of family.

CONTENTS

FOREWORD

"There are a thousand hacking at the branches of evil to one who is striking at the root." So said Henry David Thoreau—and he was right. Too many among us are distracted by the daily outrage and focused on ephemeral events. We are deceived by the media's sleight-of-hand and spend our energy fighting the wrong battles, as if we're playing a perpetual game of political whack-a-mole, exerting our effort on actions that are ultimately unproductive. Maybe the real solution is to unplug the machine and stop playing the game.

But how? Like me, I'm sure you want to fight for a brighter future for your children. You want to see our society embrace truth and stop falling prey to deceptions. You don't want to waste time hacking at unimportant branches. And that's where this book comes in.

Across the country, freedom-loving families have a sense that the foundations of our society are under siege. I regularly hear from parents who share their frustrations about how *fast* things are changing, often for the worse. It's a real-world equivalent of the recent *Floor is Lava* game show, where contestants lose if they touch the ground. Forced into jumping from one shifting obstacle to the next, every step is carefully planned lest they fall and fail. And now, with their own government recently declaring them "domestic terrorists" for speaking up in defense of their children, many parents feel like they've lost their footing without any solid ground below. The state has shown itself to be an enemy.

But this isn't new. As Connor Boyack documents throughout this important book, authoritarians and collectivists throughout world history have seen parents as an enemy—an obstacle standing in the way of their efforts to capture the hearts and minds of our children. From Stalin and Mao to Hitler, Mussolini and others, history's thugs all knew that their efforts would only succeed if they propagandized the rising generation, pushing parents aside in the process. It happens today as well, and it happens here in the United States of America. As the book explains in alarming detail, the state is a threat to our families.

But the opposite is true: our families are also a threat to the state. If we want a limited government, we need strong families that know their power and use their influence to shape the rising generation. Instead of raising snowflakes who view themselves as victims, we need to raise critical thinkers who are independent-minded and entrepreneurial. Instead of breeding dependence on government, we need to teach our children the power of problem solving and self-ownership. If we believe in freedom and want a government that honors and protects it, we need to first teach and exemplify it around the dinner table.

This is what striking at the root looks like. Consider *Children of the Collective* your operations manual explaining how to do it effectively. If you and I focus our energy on the fundamentals—building strong families with intentionality—then in the aggregate, we will shape our society and shrink the state. This lasting change doesn't come by changing a law or filing a lawsuit. It won't come by posting on social media or voting better. It comes from a series of small actions parents learn about and act upon in homes across the country. By small and simple things are great things brought to pass. Connor's book gifts parents with several powerful ideas we can act upon to do our part.

His amazing *Tuttle Twins* books, teaching children the ideas of a free society, have been read by millions. In the process, he's heard from countless very concerned parents about their kids' future and the state of our world. I hear it daily from listeners of my show as well. They know there's a problem, but many of them struggle to find solutions that make sense—and make a *difference*. Perhaps you feel similarly, wondering what exactly you can do to help improve the world around you and create better circumstances for your kids. You look around at the institutions in our society—the media, academia, and the government itself—and see not friends but foes. You feel isolated and often helpless because, after all, what can one person do?

It's time to recognize your power as a parent. It's time to elevate our families to empower our kids. And it's way past time we started playing offense instead of always being on defense. That may sound daunting, but it's doable—and it's essential if we want to protect our children from collectivists across the country who see them as little more than potential cogs in a machine to support their dastardly agenda. You feel the urgency and know that time is of the essence.

So it's time to study up on the strategy and get to work. Connor's book is a gift, perfectly timed to empower parents to take action and fight for a freer future. Drink deeply from the pages that follow, and be prepared to put these ideas into action.

Let's strike at the root together.

Glenn Beck
September 2022

INTRODUCTION

"Above this race of men stands an immense and tutelary power, which takes upon itself alone to secure their gratifications and to watch over their fate. That power is absolute, minute, regular, provident, and mild. It would be like the authority of a parent if, like that authority, its object was to prepare men for manhood; but it seeks, on the contrary, to keep them in perpetual childhood.

"For their happiness such a government willingly labors, but it chooses to be the sole agent and the only arbiter of that happiness; it provides for their security, foresees and supplies their necessities, facilitates their pleasures, manages their principal concerns, directs their industry, regulates the descent of poverty and subdivides their inheritances. What remains, but to spare them all the care of thinking and all the trouble of living?"[1]

—Alexis de Tocqueville

I GREW UP WATCHING *Star Trek: The Next Generation* each week with my parents. Before on-demand streaming ever existed, this viewing experience was a recurring event in our family's weekly schedule. When the introduction began with its familiar tune and lyrics—*Space... the final frontier...*—we would shout at the rest of our family to hurry for fear of missing anything. It was compelling TV for a family of sci-fi fans.

Our show of choice featured a number of villains: the omnipotent Q, the fearsome Klingons, and the cunning Romulans. But I distinctly remember the introduction of the most fearsome of them all: the Borg. This cybernetic creature was basically a humanoid robot—an infusion of cold technology and machinery into a warm body. Their species—if you can call it that—thrived by assimilating others into its collective consciousness. "We will add your biological and technological distinctiveness to our own," they would menacingly announce to their prey in robotic unison. "Resistance is futile."

One early episode featuring the Borg demonstrates the threat they posed. After responding to a distress call, the crew of the *Enterprise* confronts a cube-shaped vessel. The high-tech hostiles demand that the *Enterprise* lower its shields and allow Captain Picard to be transported onto the Borg vessel, threatening destruction should they not comply. Predictably, Picard refuses their demand and, after a brief skirmish in which his ship sustains heavy damage, decides to flee.

That night, Captain Picard records the following in his journal: "I have no explanation for [the Borg's] special interest in me or this ship. We continue to prepare our defenses for the inevitable confrontation, but I must admit, on this night, I contemplate the distinct possibility that no defense may be adequate against this enemy."[2]

Shortly thereafter, the Borg locate and board the *Enterprise* and abduct Captain Picard, then fly at warp speed toward Earth, intent on conquering the planet and assimilating the human race into its collective. Picard's first interaction on board their ship showcases the diverging interests of these two clashing cultures:

BORG: Captain Jean Luc Picard, you lead the strongest ship of the Federation fleet. You speak for your people.

PICARD: I have nothing to say to you, and I will resist you with my last ounce of strength.

BORG: Strength is irrelevant. Resistance is futile. We wish to improve ourselves. We will add your biological and technological distinctiveness to our own. Your culture will adapt to service ours.

PICARD: Impossible. My culture is based on freedom and self-determination.

BORG: Freedom is irrelevant. Self-determination is irrelevant. You must comply.

PICARD: We would rather die.

As a teenager, I saw the Borg as a horrible enemy devoid of any humanity. They were cold and had no personality. Their success came from suppressing the individual. I implicitly understood how awful it would be to be assimilated by them and lose my uniqueness. And yet, here, Picard expresses active resistance to any assimilation; he would rather die than lose self-determination. He saw the Borg for what they were, knew the threat they posed, and decided to fight back.

But what of those civilizations that were assimilated but knew nothing about the Borg? Consider a colony on a remote planet instantly dominated by this fearsome force of foreign conquerors. How could they successfully repel the threat against their very individuality? How could they even fight back if they didn't understand their enemy? This colony would have effectively lost before the battle even began, compelled to become part of a collective without ever standing a chance. I wondered how many (fictional) civilizations had fallen subject to these forces without understanding them?

The same pattern emerged when *The Matrix* hit theaters. I watched the movie more than a dozen times on the big screen, fascinated by its mind-bending plot and amazing special effects. Once again, the collective was presented as the enemy. In this case, it was a technological system built by artificial intelligence robots to harvest humans for their biological energy and use that product as fuel for their own machinery. The Matrix, described by Morpheus, "is a computer-generated dream world, built to keep us under control in order to change a human being into [a battery]."[3]

In this story, humankind is permanently plugged into equipment, keeping them in a constant dream state, interfacing their mind into a fantasy reality that keeps them deceitfully thriving despite having no clue that their true reality is one of captivity. Programmed into a digital collective construct that the system created and controls, individuals are unaware of the systematic suppression of their true nature. They are born into the collective and kept unaware of its reality and danger.

In liberating Neo and helping him—and the viewer—understand the threat, Morpheus explains:

> The Matrix is a system, Neo. That system is our enemy. But when you're inside, you look around, what do you see? Businessmen, teachers, lawyers, carpenters. The very minds of the people we are trying to save… You have to understand, most of these people are not ready to be unplugged. And many of them are so inured, so hopelessly dependent on the system, that they will fight to protect it.[4]

I was 17 years old when I heard these words spoken and could barely fathom how stinging an indictment they were of the world I lived in. Not only were people unaware they had been involuntarily subjected to a collective, but they were also willing to fight the very people trying to help them break free of it. It would be many years before I better understood the true prevalence of this behavior in our society—a kind of Stockholm syndrome whereby people fight their would-be liberators for trying to break their chains.

Pieces started coming together for me, like a confusing puzzle whose final image I didn't have the benefit of using as a guide, when I took up a deep interest in dystopian fiction as a young adult. Again, I noticed a pattern—helpless individuals becoming part of the destructive collective, in some cases unwittingly and in others simply unwilling or unable to fight back. Of the many examples one could share, *The Giver* comes to mind the most.

Widely praised as one of the most influential children's books, for me, it was an eye-opening echo of aspects found in our own world— an effect that dystopian authors no doubt aim for when twisting our reality just enough to present a far-fetched scenario that actually feels disturbingly familiar. Young Jonas lives in a futuristic society where no pain or fear exists. Scientific progress has allowed his society to eliminate physical differences and erase memories. War is a thing of the past, and prejudice with it; everyone acts similarly enough in the colorless world of conformity.

The Sameness is the work of the Committee, the controlling apex of the community's organizational structure that assigns spouses, children, and jobs. Sexual desire is suppressed through medication, and those who violate the rules are killed or "released." Children are born to Birthmothers, who never actually see the child, and spend their first year in the Nurturing Center with other "newchildren." The arbitrary family unit dissolves itself once the children are grown, and adults live isolated with other Childless Adults to be taken care of in the House of Old until they, too, are released.

Jonas followed a bit of a different path than the rest because he was selected to be the Receiver of Memory—a unique position for a person who, on behalf of the collective, possesses the many memories of the time prior to Sameness—when war, pain, and emotion were ubiquitous. Jonas, like his predecessors, was tasked with remembering for the purpose of helping the collective avoid repeating the supposed mistakes of the past. His blessing and his burden were to know and understand pain, suffering, happiness, inequality, and everything in between. He remembered a world prior to Sameness, and the knowledge was isolating. "The worst part of holding the memories," he said, "is not the pain. It's the loneliness of it. Memories need to be shared."[5]

He later shared some memories with Gabriel, a newchild scheduled for release (simply because of poor sleeping patterns), who Jonas illegally saves. Raised outside the system, Gabriel is freed from the rules and conformity of the society from which Jonas fled and, for that reason, can understand and tolerate the memories Jonas shares.

> "Things could change, Gabe," Jonas went on. "Things could be different. I don't know how, but there must be some way for things to be different. There could be colors. And grandparents," he added, staring through the dimness toward the ceiling of his sleepingroom. "And everybody would have the memories."

> "You know the memories," he whispered, turning toward the crib.

> Gabriel's breathing was even and deep. Jonas liked having him there, though he felt guilty about the secret. Each night he gave memories to Gabriel: memories of boat rides and picnics in the sun; memories of soft rainfall against windowpanes; memories of dancing barefoot on a damp lawn.

> "Gabe?"

> The newchild stirred slightly in his sleep. Jonas looked over at him.

> "There could be love," Jonas whispered.[6]

Like many other dystopian stories, *The Giver* portrays a rising generation unaware of what life was like before the descent into collectivist control—ignorant individuals who are unable to resist an evil they don't understand as being evil. How can a person in said situation know why to resist being controlled, let alone how? Does an animal raised in captivity understand what freedom feels like and how oppressive its chains actually are? Jonas once observed intellectually chained children in his community playing war games, mimicking an action they did not at all understand. As I read this, I couldn't help but wonder what I didn't know. What was *my* ignorance, and how was it inhibiting my individuality? How was I being held back by the culture, tradition, and society wherein I was raised?

The question gained urgency for me when I first became a father. Looking down at this helpless child, I felt the weight of my responsibility to care for and educate my new son, providing him with the knowledge and skills necessary to find his unique path in life. Whatever ignorance I personally had in my late twenties clearly paled in comparison to the impressionable being I now held in my hands. And a scary realization hit me: *my wife and I were not going to be the only ones trying to teach him*. Indeed, throughout his most formative years, we would be competing against a barrage of voices all vying for attention and affection, some of them downright destructive. To me, this marvel of creation was a unique person with inherent personality traits and predispositions I was eager to learn about—an individual whose identity would increasingly reveal itself over time. To others, he was no more than a would-be cog in their machine— another human asset to support the collective and its agenda.

The stories of collectivism and suppression of the individual I had encountered weren't just fiction—they were, in essence, creative retellings of history and current events. They were warnings to young parents like me of what to avoid for our children's sake and how to learn from the mistakes of the past to build a better future. And only once I created a family of my own did I realize how these stories demonstrated that collectivism is itself anti-family. The Borg, the Matrix, and the Committee all separated people from their natural connections and support systems. Their artificial systems of power succeeded only by disrupting natural ones. With the intention of suppressing the individual to expand their power and control, they had to undermine and eradicate the family unit.

Like the colony in *Star Trek*, unaware of the Borg's impending attack, or the newchildren involuntarily born into Sameness, I saw people all around me unwittingly integrating themselves into a larger system that depended, for its strength and success, on undermining their family. I saw fellow parents who didn't realize what they and their vulnerable children were up against. And, in that moment, I saw an obligation to spread the word, like a newly liberated Neo called to wake others up from their Matrix-induced slumber.

My takeaway from these observations is that we cannot win a war we do not know is being waged. Defending yourself against a trend or tactic you are totally ignorant of is impossible. If we want to resist a threat, we have to first know it even exists. Do parents today know the seductive lure of so-called democratic socialism and why young people claim to support it at double the rate of their elders?[7] Are today's parents—are *you*—prepared for savvy marketing messages, propaganda, and social engineering that easily capture a child's attention and often pit their wishes against those of their parents? What about academic assaults turning malleable minds away from truth, institutionalizing ignorance that can be leveraged by conniving leaders looking to repeat the mistakes of the past without being rebuffed by informed individuals who know and have learned from those mistakes? Can we recognize the calls for collectivism and their insidious subordination of the individual to the state? Do we know the nature of the state's "immense and tutelary power" that seeks "to keep [us] in perpetual childhood?"[8]

During his re-election campaign, President Barack Obama launched a fictional storybook called "The Life of Julia," depicting how the government provides Julia (and all of us) a comfortable life supported by the state.[9] From cradle to grave, Julia is supported and cared for by government programs. As a child, she benefited from government school programs; as a young adult, similar programs prepared her for college. Once graduated, she had the benefit of coverage mandates in health insurance and subsidized college loans, incentivizing her to take on easy debt. Her family planning is delayed, and her career is favored by birth control which her insurance is required to provide her, so she can "focus on her work rather than worry about her health." Her business is boosted through government loans, and her later years are cushioned when Medicare and Social Security programs provide her "monthly benefits that help her retire comfortably."

It's important to note that Julia's entire life was defined by her positive and dependent interactions with the state—a perpetual child supported by this pretend parent's power. Each step of her life was tied to a centrally planned government program. There were no parents, no husband, no relatives, no family unit, no church—just the government. These influences are subordinated, at best, to the state's direct connection to the individual; a family support system is considered competition by the state. When necessary, in an attempt not to appear so overtly anti-family, the state gives appropriate lip service while conveying what it really thinks of families. Consider the draft policy statement issued by the U.S. Departments of Education and Health and Human Services in 2016, calling for "family engagement" and "including" parents as "partners" in the education and rearing of their children.[10] "All families," it reads, "must be treated with respect and valued as experts and equal partners in their child's learning and development." We aren't in charge; our families are not our own—at least not in the government's eyes. At best, we are partners in rearing our children. How gracious of the government.

The efforts to capture a child's mind and circumvent family authority and identity are powerful and persistent. What will become apparent in this book is that these efforts are a clear and present danger to our families, yet too few parents are even aware of them. And while efforts to replace parental control with state control have appeared throughout history under many banners—totalitarianism, socialism, communism, authoritarianism, fascism, and democracy—the result is the same: the individual is dehumanized and devalued.

Parents are supplanted by the state. The many take priority over the one.

Captain Picard was able to intercept the Borg and eventually frustrate their plans to assimilate Earth because of a distress signal sent from a remote Starbase, reporting a sighting of and contact with the alien vessel. The *Enterprise*'s eventual success in saving humanity was made possible because of this warning message, affording the crew an opportunity to intercept and stop the threat. Without this warning, mankind might have been conquered by an enemy they didn't even know was seeking their destruction. Consider this book as a similar distress signal—a warning message from a friendly ally sent to caring parents so they can recognize, prepare for, and defend against the state and its diverse methods of undermining the family with the purpose of controlling the individual.

"Between the omnipotent state and the naked individual looms the first line of resistance against totalitarianism: the economically and politically independent family, protecting the space within which free and independent individuals may receive the necessary years of nurture."[1]

–Michael Novak

THE OMNIPOTENT STATE

"The most improper job of any man... is bossing other men. Not one in a million is fit for it, and least of all those who seek the opportunity."[1]

—J.R.R. Tolkien

I RECALL THE FIRST TIME I encountered Novak's quote about the family being the "first line of resistance against totalitarianism"—I was struck by its succinctness and relevance. It seemed self-evident enough, but it increased in importance for me when, just a few months later, I watched a video featuring Melissa Harris-Perry, an MSNBC commentator and professor of political science.

Recorded as a 30-second promo for her employer, Ms. Harris-Perry's remarks centered on the importance of increasing funding for public education—an odd goal for an allegedly neutral news network. But the argument behind the appeal was what caught my immediate attention:

> We have never invested as much in public education as we should have because we've always had a private notion of children, [that] your kid is yours and totally your responsibility. We haven't had a very collective notion of these are *our* children.
>
> So part of it is we have to break through our kind of private idea that kids belong to their parents, or kids belong to their families, and recognize that kids belong to *whole communities.*
>
> Once it's everybody's responsibility and not just the household's, we start making better investments.[2]

At this point in my life, I was fairly well versed in the history of various totalitarian regimes that had arisen around the world and their collectivist ideologies that sustained them until their inevitable implosion. I was also binge-reading dystopian stories and seeing similar scenarios portrayed there. Taken together, these influences made the MSNBC promo all the more alarming for me, seeing in open display the explicit advocacy for divorcing children from their families to a degree. (To what degree? In what situations? Who gets to decide? These and so many other questions were obviously not addressed.)

On its face, this plea for children belonging to communities rather than their own parents is simply incorrect. For example, Harris-Perry claims that "better investments" come when family privatization is undermined—that resource allocation will be better when collectivism coordinates the needs of children. But numerous examples bear out how wrong this is. Consider the case of the buffalo.

At one point, the American bison—or buffalo—numbered in the tens of millions, spanning almost the entire United States. Hunted for food and other resources, these animals didn't face extinction until the late nineteenth century, when heavy industrial demand for meat and hide along with widespread indiscriminate killing lowered their numbers into the mere hundreds. It wasn't intervention by the government—the "whole community," in Harris-Perry's vernacular— that solved the situation. It was a handful of private ranchers who gathered some of the remaining creatures to preserve them and grow their numbers. A century later, the privately-owned bison exceeded 160,000 in number while the community-owned counterparts had been decimated to under 10,000 in number.[3]

There's an important economic principle in play here, which is why investment in both bison and children is superior when done privately. It's called the *tragedy of the commons*, referring to a circumstance in which things in custody of the community are not sustained to the same degree as things under private custody. The private ownership of property, for example, creates incentives to save and conserve resources for potential later use. A rancher who sells buffalo products might face insolvency if his animals are exterminated, so he takes measures to protect and preserve them. But when the buffalo are publicly owned—when there is no specific owner with a vested interest in long-term success—they become overutilized because the incentive to manage them properly does not exist; each person wants to take as much as possible before the other guy does.

When everybody has responsibility, nobody does. Consider this idea as applied to another issue: police protection. It may sound odd, but the government has no legal obligation to protect people from crime. A well-known example graphically illustrates a common policy across the USA. On March 16, 1975, two men broke into a three-story home in Washington, D.C. A woman on the second floor was sexually assaulted, and her two housemates on the floor above her heard her screams. They called 911, and police were dispatched to check out the incident. After knocking on the door and receiving no answer, the police left the scene. The frantic housemates called 911 a second time. The dispatcher promised the women that help would come, but no officers were even sent. The attackers discovered the housemates, and all three women were assaulted over the next fourteen hours. When they later sued the city and its police department for failing to protect them and not even responding to their second call, the court dismissed the case, stating that the police have no duty to help individuals and only exist to provide services to the "public at large." There exists a "fundamental principle," argued the court, "that a government and its agents are under no general duty to provide public services, such as police protection, to any particular individual citizen."[4] The government "assumes a duty only to the public at large and not to individual members of the community."[5] This is not just the opinion of a few judges but a pervasive policy regarding police services throughout the nation. Individuals are left unprotected in a system that claims to only care about the collective.

Now imagine how that applies when your children become "everybody's responsibility," under the care of the collective. It's not hard to think of what this looks like because it plays out to some degree every day in government schools across the country. The individual interests and needs of your child, if enrolled in such a school, are immediately subordinated to those of the group; the teacher focuses on the average, or the lowest common denominator, rather than being able to accommodate and adapt to each child's unique abilities, interests, and goals. While you know your child's needs and can specifically and narrowly tailor your efforts to support them, a bureaucrat, administrator, or teacher cannot. Your family is equipped to nurture your child—the collective is not. Government schools offer daily tragedies of the commons for those who are willing to see them.

But Harris-Perry would have us set aside these observations and alter society such that my children, and your children, become *our* children—the responsibility of *everybody* and not just our own families. Many others agree with her collectivist approach; speaking to a group of teachers, President Joe Biden said, "They're all our children… They're not somebody else's [each parents'] children. They're like yours when they're in the classroom."[6] With responsibility over the rising generation comes power and authority; under this collectivist arrangement, we would all have the same standing to influence and indoctrinate *our* children. Can individual parents fight back when the public good and the collective supposedly require (according to those in control) that young people be taught and led to believe certain things deemed proper? Doing so would be considered selfish, moralistic, or anachronistic; after all, think the totalitarians, why should parents be entitled to be the sole deciders as to what a child is taught? What gives them that right? And how can they know better than the professionals, the bureaucrats, and the elected officials? With power comes hubris, and in a collective, this intellectual contagion can easily infect the many.

TOTALITARIAN TEMPTATIONS

Dictators throughout history have amplified the inherent tension between parents and the state in order to exert control over the minds of children. And that's why I was so disgusted with the MSNBC video. I had just recently read a quote from Adolf Hitler, the accuracy of which I initially disbelieved (having found it on the internet) until quick research proved my hunch wrong; the quote was true. Here's Hitler himself, in a November 1933 speech channeling his inner MSNBC:

> When an opponent declares, "I will not come over to your side," I calmly say, "Your child belongs to us already… What are you? You will pass on. Your descendants, however, now stand in the new camp. In a short time they will know nothing else but this new community."[7]

Years later, this infamous collectivist said, "This new Reich will give its youth to no one, but will itself take youth and give to youth its own education and its own upbringing."[8] There's danger in offering examples such as these; a logical fallacy was labeled decades ago as *Reductio ad Hitlerum*, or "playing the Nazi Card," whenever a person tries to attack another's position on the basis that Hitler or the Nazi Party held the same view. But in this case, there's no fallacy—Hitler himself verbalized the core totalitarian belief, that of capturing children's minds to secure the future of the state. Parents be damned—they would "pass on," as Hitler pointed out, and expire along with their allegedly antiquated views and loyalties. In their place would rise the new generation, educated and cultivated in a way that aligns with the collective's approval.

Simply put, collectivists such as Harris-Perry and Hitler find it difficult, expensive, or tiresome to try and persuade or compete directly against others who disagree. Instead, they circumvent the competition by devising schemes to propagandize children, substantially reducing the difficulty of expanding their ranks by enticing those who can't think critically. It's a time-tested tactic that totalitarians can't help but employ. The repressive regime in North Korea infuses such ideological propaganda into every subject consistent with the decree that children are "never to forget that they owed everything to the national leadership";[9] one math question is reflective of others: "Eight boys and nine girls are singing anthems in praise of Kim Il-sung [the ruling leader at the time]. How many children are singing in total?"[10] Widespread radio listenership (in the absence of alternatives) leads to children, and their parents, being bathed in propaganda messages, songs about the Dear Leader, military marches, and more.[11] Subjects are taught the importance of sacrifice to the state, for what truly matters to totalitarians is the many, not the few—the collective they control, not the individual with free will. Unique family and cultural diversity are a threat to the utopian schemes of technocrats who want to reimagine society in their desired image, homogenizing humanity using the engineering of the state's system. After all, what's one person in the grand scheme of the collective? "What are you?" Hitler asked the dissenting parent. You can feel his contempt and authoritarian thuggery seeping through those words.

Russia under Lenin and Stalin created a similar division. The Marxist approach to the family was one of institutional animosity; the nuclear family unit was perceived as an economic arrangement to perpetuate capitalism and facilitate the transfer of private property through inheritance, creating inequality by which some families prospered over others. The Marxist goal, therefore, was the "abolition of the family"[12] and thus to "do away with the household" so that children were not raised by their parents but instead were "supervised by trained pedagogical and medical personnel,"[13] which would create a kind of enforced equality. Women would become "the property of the nation" to undermine the relationship between mother and child—a biological connection that itself is the foundation of private ownership.[14]

One year after the Bolsheviks took power, they created the Code on Marriage, the Family and Guardianship. Among other changes, the new law established no-fault divorce and prohibited adoption; the state would take care of orphans. But in just three years' time, millions of homeless orphans were roaming the countryside; government agencies did not have the resources to take care of them. Crises such as this caused reflection and change; laws were changed, and the Marxist ideology was set aside in favor of pro-family Stalinism. Where once the nuclear family was thought to soon "wither away" as communal resources increased alongside the state's role in caring for individuals directly, it was soon recognized that the family could play a central role in the state's success—as a sort of incubator for the individual.

In 1935, Stalin declared "man the most precious resource"[15] and saw Russia ban abortion one year later, in all but exceptional cases. Party faithful soon pivoted, praising the family arrangement they had been seeking to overtly undermine. Thus did Aaron Soltz, considered the "conscience of the Party," soon praise the push for increased fertility, saying:

> Our life becomes more gay, more happy, rich and satisfactory. But the appetite, as they say, comes with the meal. Our demands grow from day to day. We need new fighters—they built this life. We need people.[16]

Motherhood became a "great and honorable duty" in the eyes of the state—it was not merely their "private affair, but an affair of great social significance"[17] of collective importance. The function of the family—and its tolerance by the state—was to facilitate procreation and care for the state's ongoing supply of new blood. A collective cannot exist, of course, without enough individuals to compose and sustain it. Families are, therefore, a "necessary evil" in the eyes of the true collectivist, for their natural byproduct is needed while their inherent authority over their children is a threat.

It is precisely that authority that is feared the most. Simply put, totalitarianism is exerting control into every area of society. As Benito Mussolini put it, "Everything within the state, nothing outside the state, nothing against the state."[18] Families seeking to preserve autonomy, propagate their own beliefs, and resist the ideological imprints of the state's propaganda machine are perceived as dissenting enemies that must be exterminated because of their potential to destabilize a delicately crafted system. This utopian scheming cannot be effectuated without the state; collectivist dreamers implicitly understand that they cannot adequately persuade the masses to adopt their proposals and change their ways. No, they must ultimately be coerced in order to suppress and stamp out resistance; political power must be acquired and applied to achieve these ends.

When utopians have the political ability to foist their schemes on the rest of us, a kind of moral terrorism ensues—and families feel the brunt of the attack. Millennia of inherited wisdom, values, and customs are dispensed with by educated elitists who replace heritage with hubristic control of what society *ought* to look like. Children are so often the direct focus of these efforts because while it is difficult to change adults' minds in any lasting fashion, it is rather easy to cultivate a child's. Dissenting parents watch in horror as the affections and attitudes of their children are trained away from them, often helpless to counteract the cultural forces drawing them down dangerous though popular paths.

But dissent is often rare; it is far more common that the cultural forces at play in a collectivist society—which is to say, most societies—are either ignored or tolerated. Accordingly, the degree to which the state assumes control is often unnoticed or excused by those subjected to it daily. Like the proverbial frog in boiling water, families progressively acclimate themselves to the environment in which they live. This new cultural tide creates a momentum of its own that presents future problems. For example, communist China instituted its infamous one-child policy—a centrally-planned regulation by the state of women's wombs, proposed and brutally enforced in an effort to curb population growth in the country.[19] The government requires the use of contraception and forcibly carries out abortions and sterilizations, in addition to other punishments, to enforce its anti-family decrees. But now, an aging population of seniors is relying on a shrinking workforce to sustain it, forcing officials to reverse the policy and allow for two children per family in hopes of bringing "an extra 30 million people into the workforce by 2050"[20] to provide the economic output necessary for the state to tax and spend on the elderly. Individuals are ignored as aggregate population percentages are treated as levers in a system created and designed by political engineers trying to shape society to conform to their ideals. But even as the policy has relaxed, many Chinese families have not taken advantage of the newfound freedom—having been so conditioned to the previous limitation and the social circumstances it yielded.[21] The decades-long cultural pressure faced by Chinese families is a stark reminder of the pressures faced by all subjects of the state and a wake-up call regarding the shocking degree to which we can become habituated to violations of family autonomy and individual rights. But the extent of such problems often becomes apparent only when something so alarming happens that we are momentarily awakened to it.

Such was the case with Alfie Evans, a British child whose tragic plight in 2017 aroused an international reaction to a clear contest between parental rights and totalitarian central planning of human life. Diagnosed with a degenerative brain disease, the young toddler was eventually being maintained only by life support, which the hospital sought to terminate. Alfie's mother and father asserted their parental rights as the primary authority over Alfie's medical care and sought to relocate him for medical treatment elsewhere. The hospital refused to grant this request and instead sought to terminate their parental rights.

The hospital made an appeal to the country's High Court of Justice to withdraw the rights of Alfie's parents and end his life. At a public hearing, the hospital's attorneys claimed that the continuing of life support treatment was not in the child's best interests and petitioned the Court to rule that it "is not lawful that such treatment continue."[22] The attorneys also argued that continuing treatment would be "unkind and inhumane."

Alfie's parents denied that things were beyond hope; his father claimed that his son "looks him in the eye" and "wants help."[23] It's not that far-fetched a claim—there are numerous instances in which medical professionals claim that a person won't survive, or can't be revived, which are proven incorrect when that precise unforeseen thing happens. Miracles happen, and no doubt Alfie's parents were hoping for one. But the Court ruled in favor of the hospital; Justice Anthony Hayden concluded that he was "satisfied that continued ventilatory support is no longer in Alfie's best interest."[24] Another court upheld the ruling, and subsequent court appeals were denied. The Supreme Court of the United Kingdom, in refusing to consider the appeal, stated that "Alfie looks like a normal baby, but... there is no hope of his ever getting better."[25]

Offers came in from other countries to provide care and support—financial, medical, and otherwise. So Alfie's parents petitioned for permission to transfer him and were denied. At all times, the United Kingdom's utilitarian approach asserted that it was doing what was in Alfie's "best interests." But who gets to make that determination, especially in a dispute as to what those best interests are—a judge who doesn't know Alfie or his loving parents? Caring parents should make such decisions, not the powerful and paternalistic state.

Such a disregard for the individual is a hallmark of collectivist systems wherein the many—or, better put, the supposed leaders of the many—claim the authority to make decisions for and enforce them upon the few. Supporters of these systems sometimes use platitudes like "the greater good" or "the general welfare" to justify their positions and disregard dissenters, but these are merely euphemisms for collectivism and its assertion of totalitarian primacy over parents. In the eyes of its functionaries and followers, the state and its professional class know best—not the untrained, unlicensed, inexperienced man and woman whose claim to authority over a child essentially rests on having had the sexual intercourse required to conceive said child. The state's message to such parents is clear: you're on borrowed time, and if you step out of line, we will step in.

THE STATE

What is the state? Here I'm not referring to American states like Georgia or Nevada, but a general term often used to describe the government, though the two terms aren't truly synonymous. The city you live in is "the state," as is Canada, the Democratic People's Republic of Korea, and Funkley, Minnesota (population: five). The state is a political organization that has two unique characteristics: it uses coercion, and it claims jurisdiction (authority) over a specific territory. Murray Rothbard, an influential economist and historian, explains further:

> While other individuals or institutions obtain their income by production of goods and services and by the peaceful and voluntary sale of these goods and services to others, the state obtains its revenue by the use of compulsion; that is, by the use and the threat of the jailhouse and the bayonet. Having used force and violence to obtain its revenue, the state generally goes on to regulate and dictate the other actions of its individual subjects.[26]

These subjects are anybody who happens to live in a geographical boundary over which the state claims authority, be it a city, a "state," or a country. If you don't do what the state's officials say while living within their territory, you will be punished. They might start lightly—a fine, community service, etc. But if you defy their authority and refuse to submit, the consequences will escalate, potentially leading to your death. Or, in Alfie's case, simply accelerating your death by trying to hasten your demise.

The totalitarianism Novak warns against is a byproduct of this institutional violence. Only the centralization of political power—whether in a dictatorship or a democracy, it doesn't ultimately differ much—gives both evil despots and well-intentioned utopian masterminds the ability to command armies, oppress the masses, and impose one set of ideas upon everyone at the point of a gun or the underlying threat thereof. But despots are inevitably dethroned; the way to enact lasting control over a society is to have those who are ruled believe in and become part of the cause of their rulers. Slavery becomes freedom, in Orwellian fashion, as the state's restrictions are thus perceived not as burdens but blessings—a tolerable sacrifice for a greater good. As Goethe said, "None are more hopelessly enslaved than those who falsely believe they are free."[27]

Because the state's success relies upon this mass social conditioning, collectivists have long focused on and sought to control the education—or indoctrination, as cynics would suggest—

of the rising generation. There's a reason why *The Communist Manifesto* controversially called for "free education for all children,"[28] and it wasn't ambivalent altruism. States everywhere have adopted the same approach, being so bold as to revealingly call it "compulsory education." The goal "has never been to instill conviction but to destroy the capacity to form any,"[29] for the state's success requires compliant citizens who from an early age have been indoctrinated to imagine they cannot survive without it. As Mencken put it:

> The most erroneous assumption is to the effect that the aim of public education is to fill the young of the species with knowledge and awaken their intelligence, and so make them fit to discharge the duties of citizenship in an enlightened and independent manner. Nothing could be further from the truth. The aim of public education is not to spread enlightenment at all; it is simply to reduce as many individuals as possible to the same safe level, to breed and train a standardized citizenry, to put down dissent and originality. That is its aim in the United States, whatever the pretensions of politicians, pedagogues and other such mountebanks, and that is its aim everywhere else.[30]

While the modern state has taken an invasive interest in children, the collectivist ideas behind this interest are certainly not new. The elevation of the state over the family—and the individual—has long been the credo of utopian architects of society. Consider Plato, who is often praised in state schools as a visionary philosopher and teacher of moral, humanitarian ideals. In *The Republic*, he calls for the abolition of private property and the family itself, arguing that both lead to envy and differences. Men and women were to both lead similar lives, including mandatory battle duty. Marriage was to be forbidden, as was rearing one's own children. Men would share all women in common, and the state would create a breeding program where only superior citizens could breed in special "mating festivals."[31] Children would be raised in state-run nurseries and taught to respect authority. It would be a "sin," he argued, "either for mating or for anything else in a truly happy society to take place without regulation."[32] Even worse, children of any inferior person and any "defective offspring" would be "quietly and secretly disposed of."[33]

This subordination to the collective is the foundation of Plato's dystopian world, and echoes of it are present today. Consider this quote from his writings:

> The greatest principle of all is that nobody, whether male or female, should ever be without a leader... he should get up, or move, or wash, or take his meals... only if he has been told to do so... He should teach his soul, by long habit, never to dream of acting independently, and to become utterly incapable of it... in this way the life of all will be spent in total community.[34]

It is this aspirational vision of community that drives collectivists in all eras to wrest control of the state in order to sculpt society in their ideal image. This aspiration assuages the collectivist's conscience by serving as the ends that justify the brutal means necessary to create and maintain such a society. Thus, the collectivist sees himself not as a monster that suppresses individual will but as an architect who, of necessity, must destroy in order to then build—a type of Thanos whose difficult calling is to enhance life by ending much of it. It is the state that provides the tools necessary to do so—and, more importantly, the legal framework to justify the required impositions on individuals whose wishes are suppressed so that collectivists might mold them like clay.[35]

Put simply, the state is the weaponization of one's ideas—allowing collectivists to impose their standard of community on the masses through violence or the threat thereof. It is a centralization of control and authority, enabling the imposition of a certain set of rules by the few upon the many. The state comes in many forms and allows no competition; it is sometimes dictatorial and, in other cases, democratic. Whoever controls it and whatever their purposes, the state is an ever-present threat to families who wish to preserve and perpetuate their social standards, education preferences, moral or religious framework, and culture—for the natural authority embodied by parents is an inherent threat to the state's success. In times of peace or prosperity, the state may ignore this threat and appear to even be supportive of parental autonomy. But deteriorating political or economic conditions can quickly change this perception and reveal the reality of the institution—its hostility toward parents, its jealous attention toward children, and its alleged omnipotence to enforce its decrees and destroy any who dissent.

OMNIPOTENCE

Novak's adjective of choice to describe the state is an intentional one; the state is not restrained, limited, or impotent. In fact, it is effectively omnipotent—or at least it asserts itself to be such. We have established that the state is a political organization that claims a monopoly on jurisdiction in a certain area. And because of this monopoly status, it rejects any claim of competition. Because it perceives itself to be the ultimate and final parental authority, families who desire something the state prohibits can be relieved—sometimes temporarily, in other cases permanently—of their legal rights to raise the children they brought into this world. Parents find themselves powerless against the state's demands to the extent that they dissent. Resistance, it seems, is futile.

The state's omnipotence produces varying responses from those who oppose it. Ask the average person on the street what they dislike about "big government," and you'll no doubt hear a wide range of answers. Some might focus on the high rate of taxes, whereas others might share concerns with spying and surveillance, socialization of health care, foreign intervention, or a long laundry list of other grievances. These and many other topics are rightly on the radar of those who feel the state has too much power, but even these limited government supporters often fail to recognize (and prioritize) one of the most troubling aspects of state power: the infringement upon families, and children more directly.

This isn't a new concern; the clash of the powerful state versus a powerless society—or the rulers against the people—has a long and storied history, especially in Western civilization. Recall, as one example, the biblical account where the people enjoyed a decentralized system of government with dispersed power that they instead wanted to concentrate into a single executive, "that we also may be like all the nations,"[36] they explained. Samuel—the tribal elder and prophet—was for good reason "displeased"[37] and warned them of the danger of their request:

> This will be the manner of the king that shall reign over you: He will take your sons, and appoint them for himself, for his chariots, and to be his horsemen; and some shall run before his chariots. And he will appoint him captains over thousands, and captains over fifties; and will set them to ear his ground, and to reap his harvest, and to make his instruments of war, and instruments of his chariots. And he will take your daughters to be confectionaries, and to be cooks, and to be bakers.
>
> And he will take your fields, and your vineyards, and your oliveyards, even the best of them, and give them to his servants. And he will take the tenth of your seed, and of your vineyards, and give to his officers, and to his servants. And he will take your menservants, and your maidservants, and your goodliest young men, and your asses, and put them to his work. He will take the tenth of your sheep: and ye shall be his servants.
>
> And ye shall cry out in that day because of your king which ye shall have chosen you; and the Lord will not hear you in that day.
>
> Nevertheless the people refused to obey the voice of Samuel; and they said, Nay; but we will have a king over us; That we also may be like all the nations; and that our king may judge us, and go out before us, and fight our battles.[38]

Samuel points out concerns pertaining to property rights and taxation (imagine a world where only a 10% tax was considered alarming!), but the core warning here involves the personal impact—the state's intentional and institutional harvesting of children for its own purposes. This is the fundamental threat big government poses—one that too few people recognize. Indeed, the "taking" of sons and daughters by political leaders has, in select cases, been extremely literal.

Malgorzata Twardecki was a single mother in Nazi-occupied Poland, caring as best she could for her five-year-old son, Alojzy. In the summer of 1943, she received an order to bring the blue-eyed boy to the town council office the next morning so that he could be sent on a holiday to improve his "health."[39] Twardecki refused to comply, leading the police to forcibly remove the boy and place him on a train with other children from the village who looked similarly. She watched the train depart without any clue where her son was being sent. "You can't imagine what it is like to have a child stolen," Twardecki later said of the incident. "We didn't give them our children. They stole them."[40] Young Alojzy, like tens of thousands of other children kidnapped in Poland, the Soviet Union, and other European countries, was "Germanized"—given a German name, forced to learn and speak only in German, given a forged birth certificate to indicate the child's German origin, and placed in "children education camps" (*Kindererziehungslager*) to either progress toward adoption into a German family or, if the child didn't demonstrate enough Germanity, to be sent to hard labor or death.[41]

The "taking" by the state was also quite literal for fourteen-year-old Lee Ok-seon, who was running an errand for her parents in what is now South Korea. Uniformed men exited a nearby vehicle, attacking and dragging her into the car. She would never see her parents again.[42] Young Lee was taken to a "comfort station"—a brothel servicing Japanese soldiers—and forced to become a prostitute by the imperial Japanese army. Like tens of thousands of other "comfort women," she endured constant rape, disease, and bleak conditions under orders of the emperor. He thought that by institutionalizing a sexual outlet for soldiers, the military might avoid atrocities like the Rape of Nanjing, where thousands of Chinese women were raped and killed by occupying Japanese soldiers. "It was not a place for human beings," Lee later recounted of her ordeal. "When the war was over, others were set free, but not me."[43]

While the state's seeming omnipotence can manifest itself in horrific fashion, as these examples indicate, it would be a mistake to think that it applies only during times of war or in limited atrocities. The Phonesavanh family's story highlights a more commonplace circumstance in which the state's power harms families. Their Wisconsin home had burned down, so the parents and their four children moved in with a relative, sharing a single room.[44] The family was fast asleep when, at 2 a.m. in May 2014, a SWAT team burst through the door and threw a flash-bang grenade, which came to rest next to the head of the family's nineteenth-month-old son. It "exploded on his pillow right in his face," his mother said. "He's only a baby. He didn't deserve any of this."[45] Costly medical bills ensued, with government officials taking the position that "it would be in violation of the law" to pay for the child's medical needs caused by government officers. As it turns out, the no-knock police raid was authorized in order to arrest a person who didn't even live in that home.[46]

The state's power is seen in compulsory schooling mandates that treat parents as criminals should they not send their child to school; in forcibly removing children from their homes for unsubstantiated allegations of abuse; in refusing to be conscripted to fight in the state's military escapades; in mandating that children's bodies be forcibly vaccinated; and in prohibiting religious worship, family gatherings, and business operations because of overblown health concerns. Its power is also seen in the routine way by which the state's agents are shielded from accountability for wrongdoing, as in the case of Amy Corbitt's ten-year-old son being shot in the back of his knee by a police officer who was trying to shoot the family's nearby, non-threatening dog. Citing the legal doctrine known as "qualified immunity," the U.S. Court of Appeals for the 11th Circuit ruled that the officer's conduct was protected by law and that the family would receive no compensation for their son's medical bills.[47]

Whether its negative impact is intermittent or protracted, the state's power poses a real threat to individuals generally and families specifically. Parents seeking to shelter their children from the influence and intentions of those in power face significant hurdles should their dissent come to the attention of authorities—for the powerful do not take well to their power being opposed.

PARENS PATRIAE

The state's apparent omnipotence is further evident in its assertion that it is the supreme or ultimate authority over our children. This stems from a legal doctrine called *parens patriae*, Latin for "parent of the fatherland." It originated in seventeenth-century common law in England, when the state intervened on the king's behalf against parents considered unable to properly care for their children. Previous to that time, as one scholar put it, "[t]he family's autonomy to do essentially as it saw fit with its children was untouched."[48] This view shielded families from state scrutiny, but it soon gave way to a more paternalistic approach from government officials looking to shield children, as they deemed best, from the corrupting influences of their parents and society. One child welfare attorney observes:

> Driven by the doctrine of preventive penology, child advocates— primarily middle and upper class white women—believed that "society should identify the conditions of childhood which lead to crime," such as poverty and child abuse and neglect, and should enact legislation to commit children found in these conditions for their protection. This goal necessitated a significant broadening of the state's authority to intervene in what were previously regarded as private family matters.[49]

Today, this legal doctrine has been expanded and institutionalized, primarily in the context of juvenile courts when state agents seek to take or transfer custody of children in cases of alleged neglect or abuse or when the government seeks to terminate a parent's legal rights to their children altogether. The courts act *in loco parentis* ("in place of the parents") to determine the legal affairs and "best interests" of the child. While it's easy to understand the thinking behind this approach in cases of clear abuse of a child, this legal power is itself abused to the detriment of parental rights and family integrity. As the U.S. Supreme Court held, "the state has a wide range of power for limiting parental freedom and authority in things affecting the child's welfare."[50] Parker Jensen's family knows a little about this.

After a tiny growth was removed from beneath his tongue, at the young age of 12, Parker was diagnosed in 2003 with Ewing sarcoma, a rare type of cancer that forms in bone or soft tissue.[51] On top of this diagnosis, the doctor suggested Parker be placed on chemotherapy immediately or face almost no chance of surviving the cancer. His parents disagreed and wanted a second medical opinion—especially after learning that chemotherapy would likely leave their son sterile— if he survived at all.

The first doctor would not relent and informed Parker's parents that if they did not begin treatment immediately, he would be forced to notify the Division of Child and Family Services to have their son removed from their custody in order to force him to begin chemotherapy. But the parents refused and moved to Idaho. A warrant was issued for their arrest after a juvenile judge in Utah ordered Parker to be placed in state custody. Heightening the tension, Parker's parents were charged with kidnapping their own son and engaging in custodial interference.[52] State authorities put out a message in the media that the parents were being abusive and medically neglectful; compliant media outlets subsequently portrayed them as stubborn and suspicious for refusing to abide by the demands of the medical and legal establishment. The state was asserting its position as *parens patriae* and therefore could not abide Parker's natural parents asserting their own inherent rights. Parker's father was subsequently found, arrested, and spent four days in jail.

Facing public outrage over the clash against parental rights, the state blinked and dropped its effort to compel young Parker to undergo the treatment he didn't want. But the message was clear to his parents: the consequences of their stubbornness would solely be on their shoulders. Authorities moved on, leaving the Jensen family to piece their lives and reputations back together. As it turns out, the parents were vindicated—years later, Parker is doing just fine, having never undergone chemotherapy and showing no sign of the illness. Had he been compelled according to the state's demands, it's quite possible that due to chemotherapy side effects, he and his wife might not have the children that are now part of their family.

Parker and his parents fought back in court, hoping to seek compensation for being subjected to the ordeal. They lost, with the matter being concluded by a unanimous opinion by the Utah Supreme Court, which held that "when a child's life or health is endangered by his or her parents' decisions regarding the child's medical care, the state may, in some circumstances, temporarily intervene without violating the parents' constitutional rights."[53] In other words, as the ultimate parent of the fatherland, the state gets to decide where danger actually exists and in which cases it can push natural parents to the side in its pursuit of expert recommendations. But Parker's case shows that the state can be wrong and that its own stubbornness can lead to dangerous consequences. Those who dissent or resist can face significant consequences.

The takeaway from all this? Parental rights can be threatened whenever the state and its functionaries think you are insufficiently caring or providing for your child. It can happen regarding medical care, education, discipline, or simple daily management of family affairs. If you behave as anything other than a model parent, the state might find a toehold to intervene and assert authority over, or even legally kidnap, your children. And while there are clear cases of abuse or neglect by parents that deserve intervention in order to protect children, this power is abused and wielded against those to whom it does not apply; Parker's parents were guilty of neither of these offenses. They merely refused to submit to the coercively backed recommendations of supposed experts who claimed to know what was best for their boy.

Those who defend the state's role in protecting children are quick to cite cases where the government acted in a child's best interest, as in clear cases of abuse by the child's parent or guardian. But beyond such limited cases, the doctrine of *parens patriae* broadly serves as pretext for each social do-gooder and central planner who thinks they know best how to shape society. It is the belief system backing up legislative proposals and bureaucratic restrictions dictating to parents how they may raise their children. In times of peace, it is a broad path with guardrails generally dictating the wide latitude within which parenting will not incur intervention; in times of tighter state control, the doctrine becomes a tightrope upon which parents must cautiously tiptoe forward, fearing that a single misstep might lead to disaster. *Parens patriae* is an ominous threat, hanging in the air, warning parents who is ultimately in charge and to whom they may be held accountable. It is a permission slip the state uses to authorize itself to intervene and put aside any parent it deems as unfit.

PROPAGANDA

The state cannot long succeed by forcibly manipulating the masses to support its goals, so it needs to "hopelessly" enslave them, as Goethe noted, by making the people *think* they're free. They must see their chains as a point of pride rather than persecution. They must find satisfaction in participating in the state's processes and programs. The state's omnipotence must be painted as a positive rather than a negative.

Like the proverbial frog in a pot of increasingly hot water, we often are so acclimatized to the status quo and its incremental modifications that we fail to realize how far things have progressed. Would Parker's parents have ever anticipated that in the so-called land of the free they could be subjected to such an assault on their parental rights? Could Alfie's parents have anticipated an altercation like the one they went through? So often, we do not realize the tyrannical potential of the state until it presents itself on our doorstep; few reading this have had the experience and might therefore struggle to envision how powerful the state has become.

I recall wondering, when I was younger, about this circumstance in the context of Nazi Germany. How could so many people have gone along for so long with the brutal regime? Were they deceived? Did they fully buy into the propaganda? Perhaps they were ignorant and could not envision that their own government had assumed—and brutally exercised—authoritarian powers. Were they aware but scared? Why is it that the masses seemingly became so heavily supportive of Hitler's statements and actions?

And then I read a book that answered my questions. *They Thought They Were Free* was written by Milton Sanford Mayer, a Jewish American journalist of German descent who interviewed a variety of Germans with different backgrounds and circumstances to better understand how Nazism became a mass movement. By the end of his project, Mayer observed that he could "see a little better how Nazism overcame Germany—not by attack from without or by subversion from within, but with a whoop and a holler."[54] He continued:

> It was what most Germans wanted—or, under pressure of combined reality and illusion, came to want. They wanted it; they got it; and they liked it.
>
> I came back home a little afraid for my country, afraid of what it might want, and get, and like, under pressure of combined reality and illusion. I felt—and feel—that it was not German Man that I had met, but Man. He happened to be in Germany under certain conditions. He might be here, under certain conditions. He might, under certain conditions, be I.[55]

The ability of the state to mold the masses into supporting its actions was something I had learned about, alarmingly, in *Propaganda* by Edward Bernays—an early twentieth-century exposé by a practitioner of political propaganda regarding "the engineering of consent"[56] by a handful of elite insiders. Bernays laid out publicly and brazenly the degree to which this intentional molding of the public's mind was a goal of government control. For example, Bernays claimed the following:

> The conscious and intelligent manipulation of the organized habits and opinions of the masses is an important element in democratic society. Those who manipulate this unseen mechanism of society constitute an invisible government which is the true ruling power of our country.[57]

The tactics revealed in *Propaganda* were among those utilized in Nazi Germany to shape what Mayer called 'German Man.' Indeed, Bernays noted that Joseph Goebbels, the Reich Minister of Propaganda for Nazi Germany, was using his material "as a basis for his destructive campaign against the Jews of Germany. This shocked me."[58] But a tool, once invented or discovered, can be utilized for good or evil at the command of its master; a match, firearm, or vehicle can serve both praiseworthy and pernicious purposes. So it was in Nazi Germany that the omnipotent state was so influential as to receive not widespread opposition and scorn from its subjects but "a whoop and a holler," as Mayer noted.

Reading the insights shared by the Germans in Mayer's book answered my questions because they revealed how willing people were to remain ignorant and believe what they wanted to believe, rather than working diligently to seek out and believe the truth. "The fact is," Mayer wrote, "that my friends really didn't know [about the Nazi atrocities]. They didn't know because they didn't want to know; but they didn't know. They could have found out, at the time, only if they had wanted to very badly. Who wanted to?"[59]

And then, the frog in the boiling water—the apathetic habituation to a changing environment. "Each step was so small," one of Mayer's interviewees explained, "so inconsequential, so well explained or, on occasion, 'regretted,' that, unless one were detached from the whole process from the beginning, unless one understood what the whole thing was in principle, what all these 'little measures' that no 'patriotic German' could resent must some day lead to, one no more saw it developing from day to day than a farmer in his field sees the corn growing. One day it is over his head."[60] He continued:

> You see, one doesn't see exactly where or how to move. Believe me, this is true. Each act, each occasion, is worse than the last, but only a little worse. You wait for the next and the next. You wait for one great shocking occasion, thinking that others, when such a shock comes, will join with you in resisting somehow. You don't want to act, or even talk, alone; you don't want to "go out of your way to make trouble." Why not?—Well, you are not in the habit of doing it…

> But the one great shocking occasion, when tens or hundreds or thousands will join with you, never comes. That's the difficulty. If the last and worst act of the whole regime had come immediately after the first and smallest, thousands, yes, millions would have been sufficiently shocked—if, let us say, the gassing of the Jews in '43 had come immediately after the 'German Firm' stickers on the windows of non-Jewish shops in '33. But of course this isn't the way it happens. In between come all the hundreds of little steps, some of them imperceptible, each of them preparing you not to be shocked by the next. Step C is not so much worse than Step B, and, if you did not make a stand at Step B, why should you at Step C? And so on to Step D.[61]

When Hitler defiantly said, "Your child belongs to us already," it was merely a statement of fact in light of this very tactic—the gradual overcoming of others' belief systems, interests, and morality through propaganda and state power. Any sensible parent would, of course, defend their child against a physical assault, but few parents have the wherewithal to observe and push back against the slow and steady assault on their child's mind. Mayer's same interviewee himself had such an experience as a father, seeing the degree to which the omnipotent state had infected his family:

> And one day, too late, your principles, if you were ever sensible of them, all rush in upon you. The burden of self-deception has grown too heavy, and some minor incident, in my case my little boy, hardly more than a baby, saying 'Jewish swine,' collapses it all at once, and you see that everything, everything, has changed and changed completely under your nose. The world you live in—your nation, your people—is not the world you were born in at all. The forms are all there, all untouched, all reassuring, the houses, the shops, the jobs, the mealtimes, the visits, the concerts, the cinema, the holidays. But the spirit, which you never noticed because you made the lifelong mistake of identifying it with the forms, is changed. Now you live in a world of hate and fear, and the people who hate and fear do not even know it themselves; when everyone is transformed, no one is transformed.[62]

It must be especially cruel to suddenly witness the degree to which your child's mind has been poisoned. Many parents might naïvely assume that their own views and ideas are being adequately absorbed by their children by merely being around them as part of a family. However, the steady, subtle propaganda of the state, combined with its influence over and outreach through schools, culture, and media, presents an extremely influential and unrelenting opposing force that will generally prevail over such parents. And in past decades, both in totalitarian regimes and "free countries," those who wish to mold the minds of the masses use children to influence their supposedly misguided parents. As one academic paper brazenly asserted, "Child-to-parent intergenerational learning—that is, the transfer of knowledge, attitudes or behaviors from children to parents—may be a promising pathway to overcoming socio-ideological barriers"[63] that the propagandists find problematic. Those barriers were, in this case, the parents' contrasting political views about "climate change." So they staged an "educational intervention designed to build climate change concern among parents indirectly through their middle school-aged children." The study found that "parents of children in the treatment group expressed higher levels of climate change concern than parents in the control group."[64] The little ones used to simply be children and grandchildren. Now they're a "treatment group" in a propaganda program—children soldiers in a war on public opinion.

War is not a word chosen lightly. After all, that's how many "educators" see their classroom—and your children. Many have long hidden this viewpoint, preferring to silently mold the minds of their captive audience. But occasionally, someone will boldly offer their thoughts publicly, as in the case of one award-winning, leftist public school teacher, Jed Dearybury, who tweeted:

> New teachers, I'm sorry if we veteran educators have misguided you about the profession. It's not about cute classrooms & trendy ideas. It's political. It's advocacy. It's the front line of battle for the future of our nation. Go no further if you're not ready.[65]

This viewpoint is not relegated to fringe teachers who see themselves as fighting some intellectual battle. Indeed, the president of the American Federation of Teachers, Randi Weingarten, said that teachers are "becoming more political, not less political."[66] But this effort to propagandize the rising generation is not a new trend; Woodrow Wilson, for example—as the president of Princeton University before he later became president of the United States—said in a 1914 speech, "I have often said that the use of a university is to make young gentlemen as unlike their fathers as possible."[67] Families who espouse values such as social conservatism, limited government, and the like might question why they send their children to institutions so dominated by those who disagree with them; in one comprehensive study, only 3.9 percent of faculty at liberal arts colleges identified as conservatives.[68] But as Dearybury's tweet suggests, the propaganda battle exists at all levels of schooling—and teachers who are more overt about their war effort don't like parents watching them go about their work.[69]

Propagandists, guided by Bernays and other masters at their craft, such as Walter Lippmann, view individuals as manipulable material—"treatment groups" to subordinate to the whims of the elite few who know best how to guide society. For his part, Lippmann felt that people were "incapable of self-rule" and that the interests and actions of the public needed to be "managed by an educated elite."[70] Bernays believed that there existed an "intelligent few" who were responsible to understand and influence the tide of history and that people were effectively too stupid to contemplate and act upon the world in which they lived.[71] Propaganda is thus viewed as necessary for "the manufacture of consent"[72] that, like the frog in boiling water, leads to Goethe's description of hopeless enslavement—a deception that would lead people to support the very manipulations imposed upon them by an unseen elite few.

WAR

Perhaps no aspect of the state demonstrates its assertion of omnipotence more clearly than war, for as Randolph Bourne once said, "War is the health of the state."[73] And since its founding, the United States of America has been at war 93% of the time.[74] The federal government maintains over one thousand foreign military bases—so many operating in the shadows that no one, including the Pentagon, knows the exact number.[75] Some half of a million troops deployed overseas are located in roughly 150 countries.[76] (Put differently, the United States has a military presence in over 75% of the countries in the world.) In the 2010 fiscal year, total "defense" spending for the American military exceeded $1 trillion,[77] a number larger than the military expenditures of all other nations in the world *combined*. Over $15 billion of that is annually dedicated to supplying weapons, training, supplies, and other assistance for the militaries of foreign governments.[78] Numerous books, such as Chalmers Johnson's *The Sorrows of Empire*, Andrew J. Bacevich's *The New American Militarism*, or Daniel Immerwahr's *How to Hide an Empire* have been written to highlight the degree to which the military-industrial complex has turned America's foreign policy into an aggressive, interventionist military machine.

Of course, war is not merely the health of the American state; countries around the world and throughout history have been subject to the same aggressive tendencies. If you define war as a conflict involving the death of over 1,000 people, then over the past 3,400 years, the world has only seen peace for 268 of them—just eight percent.[79] It is estimated that at least 108 million people were killed in wars in the twentieth century alone—and hundreds of millions throughout all of human history.[80] These aren't merely pawns in a chess game; dead soldiers leave families fatherless, brotherless, and childless (and with "gender equality" leading more women into combat roles, motherless and sisterless as well). These deep emotional scars impact countless families with ongoing trauma beyond the limited skirmishes on the battlefield. Among the negative ways in which the state can impact the family, sending individuals to kill and be killed surely ranks at the top.

In some countries, military service is mandatory, and in wartime, the state might coerce people into joining its ranks through a draft. Frequently, however, soldiers sign up voluntarily, often enticed by perks including education benefits, large cash bonuses, and more. And while heavy indoctrination takes place in the military—so that those fighting feel like they are justified when commanded to harm and kill others—many men and women question the legitimacy of the state's aggressive posture toward others.

Joe Glenton is one example of far too many. As a young boy in Great Britain, he wanted to grow up to be a soldier; as a working-class kid, he hoped to get out of poverty and find a higher purpose in life. The military "appeared to have all the trappings of a better life in pursuit of a nobler world,"[81] he later recalled. He continued:

I loved the army. I loved my regiment, my squadron and my troop. I loved the life the military offered me and wanted to stay forever. But that desire, indoctrinated into me, could not square with the reality of the wars Britain was fighting. It is like being all dressed up with nowhere to go. We were ready to die but had nothing worth dying for. Though die we did, and in the hundreds.

I see now more clearly than ever that my comrades and I were—to a greater or lesser extent depending on our jobs—hired muscle for great power. As a sagacious Vietnam veteran once told me of his time in south-east Asia: "I realised out there that I was nothing more than a redcoat" (a reference to how Americans viewed the occupying British troops during their war of independence).[82]

War involves intense dehumanization; through its propaganda, the state must persuade the masses—and more specifically, its soldiers—that those on the other end of the battlefield are not worthy of life. This is deeply destructive to the social and emotional welfare of those who find themselves as the state's "hired muscle." It is no doubt among the contributing factors causing tens of thousands of former soldiers to suffer from PTSD and subsequently kill themselves.[83]

In many cases, the state sends its soldiers to turn on its own citizens. While assault and murder are as ancient as man, the modern trend of highly centralized government has produced a system of destruction and death that far surpasses the aggregate random acts of violence individuals may commit on their own. It is estimated that in the twentieth century alone, 262 million people were killed by their own government.[84] Known as "democide" (or the intentional killing of an unarmed person or people by their government), this statistic is hard to fathom yet tragically true.

For example: the USSR killed sixty-two million of its people; China killed forty-five million; Nazi Germany killed twenty-one million; Japan killed six million; Cambodia killed two million—the list continues to include many other countries whose repressive regimes physically pitted the state against the individual. Based on the population at the time—over eleven billion people lived during the twentieth century—this means that governments killed roughly 3.7 percent of the entire human race, or a number equal to over 80 percent of the population of the United States of America at the time. If all of these bodies were laid from head to toe, and assuming an average of merely five feet in length per body, they would span the entire circumference of the earth *ten times*. Most alarmingly, governments killed more of their own citizens than that of other countries in armed conflict.

And yet, the people want peace. In America, presidential candidates have repeatedly won on a platform of peace and non-intervention. Woodrow Wilson's re-election in 1916 was largely due to his campaign slogan, "He kept us out of war," referring to his desire to avoid military conflict with Germany or Mexico. Lyndon Johnson positioned himself as the peace candidate for a win in 1964, arguing in response to the Vietnam conflict that "We are not about to send American boys nine or ten thousand miles from home to do what Asian boys ought to be doing for themselves."[85] In the following election, Johnson was defeated by Richard Nixon, who had a "secret plan" to end the Vietnam war, promising "new leadership [to] end the war."[86] George W. Bush was elected in 2000 after attacking his opponent for using "nation building and the military in the same sentence,"[87] arguing that we should "convince people who live in the lands they live in to build the nations."[88] Promising to shut down the extra-constitutional prison in Guantanamo Bay, Cuba, and withdraw troops from Iraq, Barack Obama was elected in 2008.

But in these and other examples of anti-war campaign promises and verbal concessions to non-interventionist policy by those seeking elective office, every single one of them escalated the very intervention they had harped against. Wilson led us into World War I; Johnson expanded the country's involvement in Vietnam, with some 500,000 troops sent to Southeast Asia; Nixon increased the bombings in Vietnam and spread the war to Cambodia; Bush engaged in nation-building and created a radical new interventionist doctrine on foreign policy and war; and Obama increased the commitment of troops to the Middle East, reneged on his promise regarding Guantanamo Bay, and bombed Pakistan, Yemen, and Libya. It's one thing to support peace on the sidelines, but when you find yourself at the state's steering wheel, your options for taking detours are limited; there are too many factors and influences pushing you to maintain course.

War is inherently anti-family; beyond the impact on the soldiers and their families, the killing of countless innocent people dismantles and destroys family units. Its carnage causes family separation, bombed communities become inhabitable, and familial social networks are disrupted, causing people to resettle away from their support systems. And while self-defense is obviously necessary, the story of the state is one of propaganda-fueled aggression in which boys and girls are trained and turned into mere pawns for those in power to send in furtherance of some abstract and ill-defined policy agenda.

MONEY

Before the rise of the modern state, societies experimented with a wide range of currencies to facilitate trade and preserve wealth. Past cultures have used things like metals, seashells, large stones, salt, cattle, and paper to store and exchange value. Of course, the strongest and longest-lasting asset has been gold—primarily due to its inherently low supply increase. Gold is scarce and difficult to mine, and therefore the existing supply is difficult to inflate.

This is the problem with other mediums of exchange; their ability to be more easily increased is a temptation for would-be power brokers to obtain control of the money supply and inflate it to their advantage. This corruption has also affected gold despite its superiority relative to many other assets. For example, Julius Caesar created the aureus, a coin with 8 grams of gold that was widely accepted and used throughout the continent, increasing trade and wealth for years. But when Nero later rose to power, he began clipping the coins—melting existing coins and reminting them into newer ones with less gold in them. This process allowed the emperors to effectively steal wealth from the public by inflating the circulation of coins, which devalued the existing supply—transferring wealth from the common people to those in power and their allies, who had the benefit of first using the newly minted coins before they steadily lost their purchasing power.

The downfall of the Roman Empire can be attributed to several factors, but the state's corruption of money is a primary factor affecting most others. It was the economic largess facilitated by this "easy money" that funded military adventurism, increased unproductivity, fomented political intrigue, and necessitated increasing layers of economic interventionism to address the fiscal problems it produced, including wage controls, legal tender laws, and constant debasement of the currency. But this is sadly not a trend relegated to the history books. Modern states have created *fiat* money, from the Latin word for decree or authorization. This currency has value only because the government declares it to be so and makes it official; while fiat currencies can be made more respectable by pegging them to something like gold (as was the case when they were first introduced), they become especially pernicious when disconnected from any real-world restrain on those who control the printing press.

Since the Federal Reserve was created in 1913—a central bank that effectively controls the country's economy—the U.S. dollar's value has plummeted by 94%. We know this, of course, simply by remembering our childhood. Everything was "cheaper" in decades past when, in reality, all that has happened is that the money supply has inflated, necessitating a corresponding rise in prices. And the economic destruction this process has caused is incalculable and intimately felt by families the world over who struggle to keep up. Savings rates plummet due to the Federal Reserve's artificial lowering of the interest rate, requiring parents to become speculators, seeking risky investments in hopes of preserving their wealth from currency debasement and hopefully seeing gains as well, since savings accounts yield nothing. Many adults engage in risky economic activity, overextending themselves due to "easy money" (such as buying investment properties they can't afford), only to see themselves head toward bankruptcy when market conditions change. Working parents see prices rise far faster than their wages, leading to a steady decline in their ability to provide for their families. Retirees who no longer have an income watch their savings deplete in purchasing power over time.

For many families, it's far worse; many states mismanage their economies so drastically that predictable (though still destructive) inflation leads to *hyper*inflation—where the currency is being devalued so quickly that it makes no sense to keep any, as it will be worth far less tomorrow than what it is today. Before Carine Hajjar left her home country of Lebanon, she spent her last summer nights going to the abundant restaurants in Beirut, strolling the streets filled with sleek sports cars, and visiting villages where they were greeted by friends with trademark Lebanese hospitality. "From the moment you step into a house," she wrote, remembering her visit, "there is a full mezzo set out with hummus, tabbouleh, grape leaves, nuts, and much more. Just when you're about to burst, platters of kebabs, rice, and vegetables are brought out, topped off by towers of fruit for dessert."[89] But just a few months later, the country's economy crumbled as it defaulted on its loans after years of fiscal recklessness and artificial manipulation of the interest rate, triggering hyperinflation at a rate of 462%. Families were "financially gutted… wanting for electricity and even meat."[90] Once the "land of milk and honey," Lebanon saw widespread famine; Carine's family began paying over six times their normal amount for basic groceries—if they could find them at all.

By one estimate, Lebanon was the 62nd country to undergo this destabilizing process. Under such insane conditions, people become obsessed with the economic effects of everyday life, devoting their mental and physical energy simply trying to stay above water and spend whatever they can earn as quickly as possible before its value declines the following day. People search desperately for other ways to hold on to value, exchanging their fiat money for something real. This surge in demand only makes it harder to find scarce, real resources; grocery shelves get wiped clean, and businesses collapse, unable to find the goods they need. Germany, China, the Soviet Union, Zimbabwe, Hungary, Yugoslavia, Venezuela, Bolivia, and countless other countries have seen a mass theft of the wealth of their citizens because of the manipulation of money, and the destruction of family life as intergenerational wealth is all but eliminated. Seeing the folly of having to spend armfuls (or wheelbarrows full) of paper money just to obtain some eggs or bananas, many in Zimbabwe, for example, began furiously digging massive holes in the earth in hopes of finding a few grains of gold to be used for that day's meager food supply.[91]

Sound or *hard* money insulates people against such shenanigans. Items like gold, or even Bitcoin, preserve value because their supply cannot be easily increased or manipulated. A financial system built on the integrity of money leads individuals to make rational decisions for themselves and their posterity—thinking of the long-term consequences and saving accordingly. When the state controls (and creates) money, these choices become harder to make, as the incentives to save are suppressed, and easy money incentivizes people to borrow and spend heavily and quickly. Devaluing people's earnings makes them want to spend them immediately while their value is highest, leading them to discount their future and focus primarily on the present—an economic cause with far-reaching, long-term effects. Family outlook moves from the long term to the short term, inevitably increasing welfare dependency upon the government when things go south, as long-term savings are easily eroded. As one economist wrote:

> As the reduction in intergenerational inheritance has reduced the strength of the family as a unit, government's unlimited checkbook has increased its ability to direct and shape the lives of people, allowing it an increasingly important role to play in more aspects of individuals'

lives. The family's ability to finance the individual has been eclipsed by the state's largesse, resulting in declining incentives for maintaining a family.[92]

Much has been written about the breakdown of the family. Cultural forces encouraged and persuaded more women to enter the workforce.[93] Where marriage once centered around child-bearing and -rearing, "now marriage is primarily about adult fulfillment."[94] Illegitimate births have skyrocketed,[95] and single parenting is commonplace,[96] increasing poverty and creating reliance on the state for support, which, in turn, normalizes this influence and frames it as a necessary and helpful role in individual and family life. Many scholars have lamented the trends and circumstances that have destabilized the family unit, leading to worsening outcomes for children. But extremely few have analyzed the economic factors in play—specifically, the state's control of people through control of the currency, distorting intergenerational incentives. "The well-known phenomenon of the modern breakdown of the family cannot be understood," the above-referenced economist continued, "without recognizing the role of unsound money allowing the state to appropriate many of the essential roles the family has played for millennia, and reducing the incentives of all members of a family to invest in long-term familial relations."[97]

TAXES

Paul Doumer landed in Vietnam in 1897 with a plan to modernize the area for the benefit of its French colonizers. Doing so, however, required some essential first steps, such as improving waste disposal. To that end, a sewer system began to be installed in Hanoi—yet this pipeline of human waste attracted a massive infestation of rats, which multiplied astronomically in short order. The disease-ridden pests created a huge headache for Doumer and other officials, who hired exterminators to deal with the problem. Despite killing tens of thousands per day, the team couldn't keep up with the sheer number of offspring being produced by the proliferating underground rodent community.[98]

Doumer's team came up with a plan to encourage the "capitalist development and the entrepreneurial spirit in Vietnam"[99]—they would pay one cent per rat tail. This, they thought, was a way to broadly incentivize the support of the community while obtaining evidence without having to deal with the disposal of the rat corpse. And the tails quickly came in, but French officials soon learned that the locals were cutting the tails off of rats while letting them live—allowing them to continue breeding new rats with tails to cut. Even worse, some enterprising individuals began breeding rats for the purpose, turning bare land outside the city into oceanic swells of rats piled on top of one another.

The so-called "Hanoi Rat Massacre" and its aftermath is known by another name: the Cobra Effect, a term originating in India where British rulers offered a bounty for dead cobras, leading some to breed the snakes as a steady source of income. These examples demonstrate the simple truism that people respond to incentives. Our behavior changes based on the influences, both external and internal, that might affect our choices. People who are rewarded for their work apply themselves harder. People who can subsist on free handouts from others are likely to be lazy. Children who are motivated in some fashion to learn a new skill will rise to the occasion. Employees who are paid the same no matter how hard they labor will take it easy.

Those who want to influence the actions of another need only offer new or tweak existing incentives, as the money manipulators have known for centuries. Accordingly, the family structure has long been the subject of such experiments. Sometimes this manipulation of incentives is overt, as in the case of some jurisdictions where the fertility rate has fallen so low that central planners conjure up ideas like a "baby bonus"[100] to pay parents for procreating—or, more aptly, for providing the government with future taxpayers to help sustain its costly programs. But these direct incentives are less common; they are more of a visible shove, pushing parents into a particular course of action, than the less visible nudges that are the more frequent tool of central planners.

Indeed, the "nudge" is perceived as "legitimate for choice architects to try to influence people's behavior."[101] So argued Cass Sunstein, the controversial regulatory czar under President Barack Obama who, prior to his time in government, suggested that officials should "cognitively infiltrate" groups that held politically incorrect views in order to then discredit them.[102] Sunstein's book, appropriately named *Nudge*, makes a case for propaganda to manipulate behavior by using what he calls "libertarian paternalism"—establishing certain appropriate choices for the people to make (hence the paternalism aspect) and maintaining their ability to choose their preferred option (which is supposedly libertarian). These "choice architects"—a surely Orwellian description that Bernays referred to as the "invisible government"—nudge people in a certain direction by putting boundaries around the choices available to them. This allegedly libertarian approach provides people the same amount of freedom that rats in a laboratory maze have—free to choose certain options without knowing that they're actually being experimented on by others with more knowledge about the circumstances in play.

Beyond monetary manipulation, it is often through tax policy that these nudges have been orchestrated against families by the omnipotent, quietly encouraging changes in family size or greater spousal independence. Consider the case of Sweden, where in a "pursuit of an egalitarian goal" to liberate women from their alleged "economic dependence"[103] on the family, the government reformed the tax structure in 1971 to eliminate joint tax returns, where families reported shared income and expenses and were treated as a single unit.[104] This change effected the goal of its architects to "eradicate the principle of the man as a chief wage earner in the family" and to pursue the "abrogation of the housewife system."[105] As a result of this change, women who wanted to be mothers and housewives were financially disadvantaged because "her husband's income was taxed at the full amount rather than being reduced because of her dependency."

It is no surprise that this prompted a surge in women entering the workforce, reducing the number of housewives from 1.3 million in 1950 to just 52,000 in the entire country six decades later.[106] This trend of both parents working outside the home continued to such a degree that when a Swedish journalist sought out a housewife for a newspaper article he was writing in 2010, he could not locate a single one.[107] Despite a majority of women wanting to be a housewife and spend more time with their children, "the reason why so many women choose to work is a financial question."[108] They are incentivized and act accordingly.

Today in Sweden, "the median voter is a woman who works for the public sector, and around two-thirds of the electorate draw most of their income from the state, either because they work in the public sector or draw benefits from it."[109] The heavy social welfare spending is funded through a high rate of taxation, which itself incentivizes a dual-income approach to parenting wherein both father and mother enter the workforce to foot the bill. But taxes are merely a function and form of state intervention, a conduit through which individual behavior is modified. Thus, the outcome for families is more than financial, as in the words of one of Sweden's leading economists:

> The high marginal taxes and the production of public services cause the family to more and more focus on the care of objects, while public institutions, to an increasing extent, take over the care of people, an occupation earlier regarded as the specific duty of the family. In a welfare state of the Swedish type it is not the corporations that are socialized, but the family, or more correctly, many of the traditional functions of the family.[110]

The state's taxation regime, and the resulting financial benefits regurgitated among the people, are among the contributing factors for the decline in the fertility rate. For example, in the United States, programs such as Social Security and Medicare have crowded out—suppressed—the natural incentive to raise children as a hedge against poverty later in life.

> Most workers foresee getting enough support from the public retirement system to stay out of poverty when they get older, making it less likely that they will have to call on direct aid—either in cash or in kind—from their own children. Recent studies… show that Social Security and Medicare actually reduce the fertility rate by about 0.5 children per woman. In European countries, where retirement systems are larger, the effect is closer to one child per woman. In other words, without government-run retirement systems, both the U.S. and Western Europe would have fertility rates of about 2.5 children per woman—safely above the population-replacement rate—rather than their actual rates of about 2.1 and 1.5, respectively.[111]

Fundamentally, taxes take money from families that would have been available for basic necessities, education, and opportunities for entrepreneurship and investment. They are used by the state—after siphoning off a significant portion—to provide benefits to the very people from whom they were taken. Both the taxes and the resulting benefits, such as parental leave and childcare, act as incentives that alter family decisions on when to have children and how many to have. They incentivize parents to delegate the care of their children to unrelated strangers and encourage mothers to enter the workforce in pursuit of a second stream of family income.

The state's omnipotence compels parents to pay whatever is demanded of them, for dissenters are taken from their families and thrown in jail. It's an extortion fee families must pay in order to avoid the state's wrath, plundered from their pockets and returned to them in the form of programs and services they may not need nor use. As the French economist, Frédéric Bastiat said, "When plunder becomes a way of life for a group of men in a society, over the course of time they create for themselves a legal system that authorizes it and a moral code that glorifies it."[112]

...AND MORE

Ora Cook received an inappropriate phone call one evening in June 1964 and pointed the finger at fifteen-year-old Gerald Gault, a neighbor boy. The sheriff of Gila County, Arizona, took Gerald into custody without notifying his parents. His mother returned home that night to find her son missing, and after finally locating him at the jail, she was told she could not take him home.

Gerald insisted that the deed had been done by a friend of his, but the judge kept the boy in custody for several more days, though he had not yet been tried in court. Ms. Cook, the key witness in the case, did not offer testimony at trial, yet despite the lack of evidence, the judge sentenced the boy to confinement at the State Industrial School (essentially a prison for youth) "for the period of his minority"—until he turned twenty-one, six years later. Had he been an adult at the time of his supposed crime, his conviction would have involved a maximum sentence of two months in prison and a fine of $5 to $50.[113]

Imagine the state eliminating a young person's entire juvenile life over a prank phone call (one that he potentially didn't even do). Consequences such as these are part and parcel of the punitive approach taken against parents and children, often with little regard for the damaging impact such actions will have on the social and emotional welfare of the family and its participants. The sheer power of the state, and its willingness to use it, should cause families to seriously consider their place in relation to it. But the aforementioned examples of the state's omnipotence are merely a few of many.

Free-Range Parenting. Or, as our parents used to call it, parenting. Across the country, parents are arrested, charged with neglect, and worse, for letting their children experience reasonable independence, such as playing at a park alone or walking to the store without supervision. The Meitivs are one family among many who fend off allegations of neglect and threats of having their children taken because of this parenting style and a complaint filed by a disapproving neighbor. For their part, the Meitiv children, ages ten and six at the time, were in state custody for five hours after being picked up by police while walking home from the park.[114] The family later won their lengthy and costly legal battle to clear their name. Not all are as fortunate.

Vaccinations. State laws generally compel parents to inject their children with a wide range of chemical concoctions as a prerequisite for participating in state schools they already are taxed to support. Some jurisdictions are more flexible in allowing exemptions than others, but this mandate is not without risk. Many children have been harmed by vaccinations, so much so that the state provides vaccine manufacturers with legal immunity to exempt them from liability for any such harm and quietly provides payouts to families of injured vaccine recipients, totaling over $4 billion.[115]

Compulsory Education. Horace Mann's common school concept in the 1830s was designed to reclaim children from their diverse family backgrounds and values to instead create a unified identity—a common philosophy "to be shared by Americans of every background and persuasion."[116] Mann was responsible for the country's first compulsory schooling in Massachusetts,[117] which soon spread to other states. At various times and in different countries, homeschooling— the natural right of families to educate their own children—has been criminalized by removing exemptions from the compulsory education law that mandates children attend government school.

Welfare. Social service programs are predicated on the idea of a "safety net" for the most vulnerable in society who would suffer or die without such help. But historically, private charity "dwarfed the efforts of formal social welfare agencies"[118]—until the state aggressively expanded its role and made charity "as cold as the payment of taxes."[119] The poverty rate was declining until the War on Poverty began in 1964, leading the government to expand its efforts further following the New Deal.[120] Many people, responding to incentives, simply find themselves better off living on welfare support than having to work. This unnecessary dependence upon the state, for all the other havoc it wreaks, reduces educational and economic opportunities for children.

Occupational Licensure. Having to obtain a permission slip from the government in order to legally work in one's chosen profession directly undermines the financial health and overall stability of affected families. This is especially true for immigrant professionals who possess experience in their line of work—say, a barber or an attorney—which is not recognized by the government they now live under. The state forces such individuals, if they wish to work in the same profession, to start over in the education system, taking classes to learn things they already know before moving into entry-level positions in a field in which they already have mastery.

Abortion. There are few things as destructive to families than giving legal sanction to snuff them out before they start. The state's explicit permission to kill one's offspring has tragic consequences in the case of the killed baby, the consenting mother, and certainly in the aggregate for families overall. The world has been denied the contributions of countless individuals as a result of current abortion laws. The matter is made worse when the state financially subsidizes such activities, providing taxpayer-funded assistance to those who wish to end their baby's life before it officially begins.

Marriage Licensure. The basis for beginning to require state permission to marry was specifically to enforce prohibitions against white people marrying Black people, "mulattos," Japanese, Chinese, Indians, Mongolians, or Filipinos.[121] Laws in many of the states had long been in place to outright prohibit such mixing of the races. Maryland was the first[122] to enact prohibitions in 1664. In Virginia, interracial marriage was banned in 1691.[123] By becoming the arbiter of marriage and imposing a licensure requirement, the state was able to "prevent illegal and unlawful marriages."[124] And while the early decades of marriage licensure routinely facilitated denial to people of different races, it is not entirely relegated to history; one interracial couple in Louisiana was denied permission to marry as recently as

2009. "I'm not a racist," the license-denying judge said. "I just don't believe in mixing the races that way."[125] Many families have been criminalized by the state—as remains the case today, for example, with polygamous families—causing a direct assault upon people's personal choices and the families they wish to form.

Immigration. The state's rigid approach to immigration laws is harmful to families by giving its blessing to some members while denying passage to others. Many family members find themselves separated by invisible lines on a map, arbitrarily kept apart because they lack legal permission to be together. The harm to families is even worse for those who attempt to disregard such laws in hopes of economic opportunity and familial cohesion, as in the case of the federal government's controversial separation of parents and children who had crossed together into America's southern border during the summer of 2020. Some parents were not told that their children were even being taken; in one case, Border Patrol agents told a mother they were taking her daughter to be bathed, but they never returned her to her mother.[126]

These and many other examples illustrate the relative omnipotence of the state. Sometimes its power is exercised cautiously and considered reasonable—especially by unaffected onlookers. In many circumstances, the state's power is culturally accepted and popularly supported—and, when exceeding conventional bounds, it is typically excused away with all kinds of mind-bending reasons because, surely, the person must have done something to deserve their fate.

Despite the majority generally siding with the state, there are always the affected few whose desire for independence and deviation from cultural norms provoke its ire. Cases of potential or actual conflict with the state present another lens through which we might assess the harms that can come to family members individually, and families collectively, because of the state and the aims of those who control it. We measure the strength of something by determining how easily it can oppose something else.

Who can stand up to this power? How do we shield ourselves from an attack by a seemingly omnipotent foe? Before we address such questions, we must first understand how exposed—how "naked"—the individual is by comparison in order to then fully appreciate the importance and relevance of the family.

THE NAKED INDIVIDUAL

"The whole history of the progress of human liberty shows that all concessions yet made to her august claims, have been born of earnest struggle… If there is no struggle, there is no progress. Those who profess to favor freedom, and yet deprecate agitation, are men who want crops without plowing up the ground. They want rain without thunder and lightning. They want the ocean without the awful roar of its many waters.

"This struggle may be a moral one; or it may be a physical one; or it may be both moral and physical; but it must be a struggle. Power concedes nothing without a demand. It never did and it never will."[1]

—Frederick Douglass

MAX EBEL WAS A MASTER SCULPTOR and an excellent musician. A German, he was conscripted to fight in World War I. While fighting in France, he once was in hand-to-hand combat, forced to kill another man to avoid being killed himself. This took a toll on Max, and each year he would become "sullen and depressed"[2] leading up to the anniversary of the horrible event. This experience and its lingering effects no doubt had an impression upon his children later in life. It led to his son, Max Jr., becoming a pacifist. Max Jr. loved his involvement with the Boy Scout organization, an interest shared by hundreds of thousands of his young German peers. Though only a few years old, the organization had quickly risen in popularity, and many of Max Jr.'s happiest memories came from his participation with this group.

When Adolf Hitler rose to power in 1933, he began attacking, and later prohibited, groups like the Boy Scouts that competed against the youth arm of the National Socialists, later nicknamed the "Hitler Youth." The pressure had been rising, yet Max Jr. refused to join—even in late 1936, at age seventeen, when all boys were required to join, and their existing organizations were forcefully merged into the state's youth apparatus. A few weeks later, several nationalistic teenage boys confronted Max Jr. in a knife fight; he was stabbed badly in the hand, then grabbed the knife and slashed the other boy's face. He escaped, but life had become dangerous, so he fled to America.[3]

Nazi Germany was not the only place where children were seen "not just as the recipients of nurture, but as an audience for political ideas."[4] The Soviet Union saw similar restrictions, including banning the Boy Scouts as the "Young Pioneer" organization—a branch of the Communist Youth Movement—tightened its grip over the rising generation, inculcating them with Leninist propaganda. The state subsequently exerted its influence "in every other area of work with children as well, from literature and arts to education."[5] Every channel of communication was utilized to reach and teach children the ideas favored by the state's ruling class; censorship banned conflicting ideas, and propaganda mandates ensured that every child could be influenced by those in power.

It's potentially problematic to share examples such as these because they are often seen as unrelatable; surely, democracies share nothing in common with dictatorships, right? But there is danger in dismissing these cases and believing that other governments and cultures are not also collectivist with similar dangers, albeit to a different degree. Sometimes, in the potent extremes, we see the strongest warnings of elements present in our seemingly stable status quo.

It was Hitler who gave voice to the trend that collectivist central planners had long understood: "He alone who owns the youth, gains the future."[6] The omnipotent state thus takes an interest in the rising generation for its own sake, imposing its power and influence to whatever degree is most possible and practicable. The subject of this outreach campaign is the "naked individual," as Novak called it—an impressionable boy or girl who, like a sponge, soaks up whatever he or she is exposed to. Children are, to some degree, a *tabula rasa*—a blank slate onto which others can draw their desires, like a canvas to be painted by others in control. In a state of nature, the young must of necessity rely upon their elders as trusted authorities to pass down important information—essential dos and don'ts to guide the curious but ignorant individual. And the omnipotent state offers an abundance of authorities to complement (or, rather, compete against) the natural authority of parents. Thus children take as truth what they are taught by "teachers" and give due deference to decrees from politicians, orders from doctors, and commands from cops. They don't know any better, of course; the naïveté of the young is precisely why they can so easily be molded.

To be "naked" in this context is to be ignorant, defenseless, vulnerable, and persuadable. The weak nature of the individual child is precisely why the strong hold such sway; without assistance from others, the exposed child is unable to protect themselves from forces that would capture and control them. And obviously, the state is looking to the young because of the opposition of (some of) the seniors who would know better. Hitler again pointed out a trend of which we must beware:

When an opponent declares, "I will not come over to your side," I calmly say, "Your child belongs to us already… What are you? You will pass on. Your descendants, however, now stand in the new camp. In a short time they will know nothing else but this new community."[7]

It is hard to change an adult's mind, and while brute force can create submission, that only lasts for so long. Teaching a new idea is easier than undermining or replacing an existing one. So the best chance that the state has for long-term domination is to convince its subjects that it is not brutal but benevolent. And the easiest way to persuade a populace to adopt a new perspective is to propagandize the youth. Children are taught racism, xenophobia, tribalism, and more—taught that the "other" is the enemy and that the state is their protector. These are learned behaviors and manufactured opinions—some of the state's many efforts to subdue its subjects into seeing it not as the aggressor but as their guardian angel against boogeymen, real or invented. Individuals are often drawn to this narrative as the state gives them an identity—a shared bond with others around which they can rally against the supposed "other team" that must be defended against or defeated. But the costs of assuming the state's identity as your own are high. "Man is born free," the philosopher Jean-Jacques Rousseau once said, "and everywhere he is in chains."[8] The strongest chains are not those that are reinforced with hard metal and impossible-to-pick locks, but rather those that are perceived not to even exist. The naked individual remains weak so long as she is unaware of her nakedness and the state's control over her. Strength is most powerful when it doesn't even have to be used.

But why does the state want us to remain naked? The answer is simple: political power is relative. Like a zero-sum game, as our power grows, that of the state decreases. Conversely, if we lack power, the state is able to wield substantial power. As we will later see, it is the family unit that can shield the naked individual and protect and prepare children for an adulthood that involves asserting and protecting one's power over oneself. Imagine a world where families were fully able to care for their members. This power to provide would strongly limit, if not eliminate, the power of the state to create welfare programs, enrich countless bureaucrats to manage them, tax the population to fund them, and skew economic incentives that would encourage more people to seek welfare over work. On the other hand, families who do not or cannot provide for their members give an opening for the state to intervene, set such precedents, and wield this power. As another example, parents who shirk their responsibility to educate their children and instead delegate it to the state surrender their power and place it in the hands of professional propagandists, such as the teacher who considers his classroom the "front line of battle for the future of our nation."[9] Those in power prefer weak people "in perpetual childhood,"[10] as de Tocqueville pointed out, so their claim to rule is not contested and so they can cultivate continued support to preserve their power. To expand its influence, the state must therefore reduce our own.

The comparative nakedness of the individual, contrasted against the state's seeming omnipotence, appears in four primary areas: physical, social, spiritual, and intellectual. Understanding how the family institution can interpose itself to protect against and remedy a child's proverbial nakedness first requires that we explore each of these areas of life.

PHYSICAL NAKEDNESS

Have you ever purchased a new car, and then you suddenly see the same car over and over again as you drive around town? It's happened to me, but this phenomenon certainly isn't limited to vehicles. When my children were young, I found myself paying far more attention to news stories involving little kids; these stories hit closer to home as I wondered how I would feel if something happened to my little ones.

I remember first hearing the story mentioned earlier of a no-knock warrant served by police in Georgia, where officers threw a flash-bang grenade into a home, landing in the portable crib of 19-month-old "Bou Bou," as his family called him. The boy was so injured by the explosion that he was put into a medically induced coma. He spent weeks in a burn unit, undergoing multiple surgeries which the county refused to pay for (claiming "it would be in violation of the law"[11] to do so). As I read about this story, I tried to contemplate how this boy's parents were feeling and what they were experiencing. Here, the state directly harmed—and nearly killed—their innocent child and, to make matters even worse, refused to pay for the consequences of their actions. I wondered how I would react in this situation. I was definitely angry, perhaps because there were so many of these stories happening. There was a steady stream of news stories of children being killed throughout the Middle East, by soldiers invading their community or from drones in the sky. Countless more children were displaced from their homes due to the U.S. government's economic sanctions and foreign policy decisions. I watched videos of impoverished families suffering in various countries from the fiscal recklessness of the state, with the sad faces of malnourished children on display. And as many families sought a better life in the United States, they were punished for crossing an arbitrary line and separated from one another, with the parents punished and sent home, while their children were kept behind and "taken care of—put into foster care or whatever,"[12] as the White House Chief of Staff once put it. Officials said there were no plans to reunite these children with their parents because "it would destabilize the permanency of their existing [state-mandated] home environment."[13]

I also saw many other people turn off the TV or scroll past the photos and videos of the suffering children. I get it—it's tough to see. It's easier to ignore. But that's not my nature. In fact, it's what drove me into political activism to begin with. On March 29, 2008, a phone call was made by a person claiming to be a sixteen-year-old girl named Sarah who had been abused, physically and sexually, at a polygamous community in Texas known as Yearning For Zion. Based on that call, a massive group of law enforcement officials descended upon the community—SWAT teams with snipers, police officers with automatic weapons, helicopters, and armed personnel carriers.[14] All because of Sarah's tip, 416 children were forcibly removed from their families. But there was no Sarah—the call was a fake. It was placed by a much older woman, Rozita Swinton, who had previously been arrested for making hoax calls posing as abused and victimized girls.[15] But that didn't matter to government officials. They argued that the children were being removed because of the *potential* for abuse in the future.

These children were placed into a foster care system in Texas, where, at the time, children were four times more likely to die than children in the general population.[16] In 2004, a few years prior, 100 foster children in Texas received treatment for poisoning from medications, 63 received medical treatment for rape occurring while in the foster care system, and 142 children gave birth while in the system.[17] The state's removal of children over an alleged "potential for abuse in the future" didn't stop their placement into a far more dangerous environment—and all because of a fake call.

I was in another state, reading online reports of these events in real time. I was fixated, horrified at the brazen exercise of rubber-stamped government power separating these families who were not individually suspected (as supposedly required by the Fourth Amendment) of any criminal wrongdoing. But while I was horrified, I was also politically ignorant; as a recently married, young web developer, I had no clue what I could do about it. I ultimately decided to start an online petition for the return of the children to their mothers—a form of online activism that, in 2008, was still new and underutilized. This petition quickly made the rounds with my limited marketing abilities helping, and we soon had over one thousand signatures. That led to media attention, including my first TV interview and letters from elected officials saying they were monitoring the situation but felt like they couldn't do anything about it. Eventually, most of the children were returned, but only with conditions from the judge that authorities be allowed to make unannounced examinations of the children without parental interference, that the parents had to take parenting classes, and that the families could not leave Texas. And I was left to wonder: if hundreds of kids can be taken from their parents over a mere "potential for abuse," placed in dangerous circumstances, and harmed without consequence… what's to stop the state from ever doing that to my children? And how would that actually feel, to be ripped away so easily from your loved ones—to feel so vulnerable and helpless when pitted against armed agents of the state?

Because children are vulnerable by nature, they must rely on adults for their care—not only to clothe their physical nakedness but to protect and provide for them as well. The most basic role of a parent is to support their children with their physical needs, such as shelter, food, and clothing. But because of its size and scope, the state can easily deprive individuals of these things, even if only inadvertently. For example, while children are rarely directly targeted for democide[18] or in war, they are among the "collateral damage" that is so easily ignored or dismissed by the perpetrators—accidental deaths that are excused away in pursuit of a desired policy objective. Children who suffer are a rounding error, at best, in the state's mind.

This stark reality of our physical powerlessness, when pitted against the power of the state, is something that Brandon Bryant learned the hard way because he was guilty of participating in the problem. As a drone operator for the U.S. Air Force, Brandon's job was to guide the bombs that fell onto people half a world away. He was responsible for 13 known deaths and his squadron for 1,626, including women and children.[19] From the safety of his control station in Las Vegas in February 2007, he was zoomed in on a building that was about to be demolished by a laser-guided bomb he had deployed. He didn't know who was inside or what they had done to deserve death. He was simply ordered to pull the trigger. Moments before the bomb made contact, a child ran into the building, ostensibly after hearing the incoming missile and hoping to seek shelter from its destruction. The child was killed, along with anyone else inside. Panicking over what had just happened, Brandon turned to his peers, who dismissed his concerns, suggesting that it was merely a dog— something he confirmed was not true. A child had died.[20]

That child was one of many who have died due to decisions made by faceless bureaucrats in remote locations, unaware of and unconcerned with their existence. More than a thousand children have been killed in Syria by U.S.-led forces. U.S. coalition forces in Iraq have killed another thousand. Twenty-four children have been confirmed killed in Afghanistan, and U.S. drone strikes in Pakistan have killed two hundred. As atrocious as these numbers are, they are far fewer than the number actually killed due to poor data keeping and record management.[21] A political scientist who tracks such casualties notes: "Most children killed and injured directly by U.S. forces and their allies were killed the same way as their parents: they died when bombs fell; when they were caught in 'cross-fire'; shot in night raids; shot at check-points and run over by U.S. convoys who speed through the streets and roads."[22] Children who are fortunate to survive are, of course, still subject to a wide range of harms, including emotional trauma, restricted education options due to schools being destroyed or teachers killed, displacement, decreased access to medicine and treatment, death of parents or other family caregivers, and more.

It is also children who fight such wars. If "war is the health of the state," then young people are its nutrients. The rising generation is required to sustain the state's military strength. So it goes to great lengths to encourage their enrollment willingly through propaganda and incentives while relying on conscription to coerce youth into servicing its needs if volunteers come up short. Over two dozen countries actively enslave[23] their youth in this manner and punish those who evade what Communist China, in its constitution, calls "a sacred duty of every citizen… [and] an honored obligation… to perform military service."[24] Singapore mandates the service of citizens at age sixteen and criminalizes not only those who refuse to be conscripted but also anyone who encourages others to refuse.[25] In Israel, both boys and girls over eighteen are compelled to enlist; youth who resist are branded as traitors and imprisoned, including in solitary confinement.[26] Children are the raw material for warmaking—a batch of "human resources" to be used as the state sees fit.

Physical freedom implies property rights; we own ourselves and can control our bodies as we see fit, provided we do no harm to others. But this freedom is a threat to the state's supposed supremacy; therefore, this freedom is not tolerated. And the state positions itself as *parens patriae*, the ultimate controller of our children's bodies, too. There's a reason that dystopian fiction typically lacks any semblance of strong families; the state's awful authoritarianism requires that it be the beneficiary and custodian of children. Babies are to be bred for the state's success. In Ayn Rand's *Anthem*, the state arranges an annual Time of Mating in which young adults are assigned as couples by the Council of Eugenics. "Children are born each winter, but women never see their children and children never know their parents."[27] Aldous Huxley's *Brave New World* saw children manufactured in sterile State Conditioning Centers, genetically engineered in a society with no families whatsoever to become docile creatures resigned to their predetermined social status—an operation "undergone voluntarily for the good of society."[28] Lois Lowry's *The Giver* has reproduction assigned to Birthmothers who "never even get to see newchildren." Each Birthmother has three babies over three years and is then assigned to "hard physical labor"[29] for the remainder of their lives.

Over and over again, these intentionally awful futuristic snapshots depict children being cultivated, their bodies to be controlled for the state's purposes. As a parent, this horrifies me; I didn't start a family and have children with my wife only for them to be subordinated to the state. I want my children to be free. But I must concede that compared to the power of the state, my children are proverbially naked—vulnerable to harmful exposure from which they lack adequate protection, especially if left to their own devices without my parental interventions. Absent those interventions, such as they may be, my children would be a mere cog in the state's machine, as unable to resist as the millions of other children throughout world history who have been molded into the state's desired condition, to be used or tossed aside at its pleasure.

SOCIAL NAKEDNESS

Jan-Erik Olsson, a repeat offender of armed robberies and other violent crimes, was out of prison on parole on August 23, 1973, when he entered a bank in Stockholm, Sweden, with the intention of robbing it. After police were called, Olsson took hostages and remained in the bank's vault for six days, demanding that a fellow bank robber be released from prison to join him, which the government granted in hopes of establishing more communication. Olsson called the Prime Minister and threatened to kill the hostages, grabbing one forcefully, causing her to scream as the call ended. On a subsequent phone call, Kristin Ehnemark, one of the hostages, told the Prime Minister, "I think you are sitting there playing checkers with our lives. I fully trust... the robber[s]. I am not desperate. They haven't done a thing to us. On the contrary, they have been very nice."[30] After the hostage situation was resolved—police pumped tear gas into the vault, and the perpetrators quickly surrendered—the hostages and their captors embraced and shook hands. Two female hostages cried to the police, "Don't hurt them—they didn't harm us."[31] Astonishingly, the hostages even raised money for the legal defense of their captors.[32]

Just a few months afterward, two men and one woman broke into the San Francisco apartment that twenty-year-old Patty Hearst shared with her fiancé, threatening them with firearms. Hearst—the granddaughter of the wealthy publishing magnate William Randolph Hearst—was blindfolded, gagged, and thrown into the trunk of a car. Her captors were members of the anti-capitalist revolutionary group Symbionese Liberation Army (SLA), whose hideout was nearby. Initially, her captors hoped to use the Hearst family's connections to secure the release of two of the group's imprisoned members. When that failed, the SLA demanded that the family make a massive donation to the poor. As the demands were made, Hearst was kept bound and blindfolded in isolation for nearly two months as she was lectured about the group's beliefs. She was abused and coerced to record messages to alienate her family. She was subjected to psychological conditioning, and it worked—on April 15, 1974, Hearst wielded a semi-automatic firearm alongside her captors during a bank robbery.[33] Weeks later, she shot an automatic firearm several times toward a store manager who was trying to stop an SLA member from stealing from his store. She assisted in a carjacking, abducting the owners. Hearst also helped make explosive devices intended to kill police officers.[34] In short, she had been brainwashed into becoming a willing accomplice in the group's destructive activities. When finally arrested, nineteen months after her kidnapping, she asked her attorney to share a message publicly on her behalf: "Tell everybody that I'm smiling, that I feel free and strong and I send my greetings and love to all the sisters and brothers out there."[35]

Known as Stockholm syndrome—named for the Swedish incident mentioned above—the tendency to develop empathy for one's captors and controllers offers a frightening example of psychological manipulation. Naturally, we revile such circumstances and decry the intentional manipulation of people to believe and act in a way that is clearly against their own interests. And we no doubt wonder how people can be led to the point of learning to love their proverbial chains and those who set them. Perhaps we feel that in similar circumstances, we would resist, or that isolated incidents such as these don't have any significant bearing on broader trends that might indicate that we, too, fall prey to propaganda tactics that push us to empathize with those in power over us. But if victims can be persuaded to praise their predators in a short amount of time, then perhaps we might be conditioned over longer periods of time, under a sustained effort, to support the state?

At its core, this question is fundamentally about who we consider ourselves to be. Patty Hearst came to feel a part of the SLA and adopted the group's beliefs, dress, vernacular, and mannerisms. Each of us develops an identity—a set of relationships that helps define and describe us. We might be members of a church, residents of a neighborhood, part of a family, employees of a company, or members of a team. The social relationships we develop enable us to identify ourselves and help us understand who we are. As social creatures, we crave identity; we are taught to root for the home team and feel patriotic feelings about our country. We crave being in the cool kids club and feeling connected to others.

Above all, our family provides us with an immediate and inherent identity. We are a child and typically a sibling as well. Through our ancestry, we're connected in a chain of human relationships to grandparents, great-grandparents, and beyond—with aunts and uncles, cousins and more. We belong to something greater than ourselves, just as a single thread is interwoven into a larger tapestry that creates meaning and beauty. A naked individual in a social context is, therefore, one who has not discovered this deep connection that helps define them; a toddler, for example, does not fully understand its natural family relationships or personal identity that stems from them. Orphaned children without this connection yearn for it, hoping to better understand themselves by learning about their parents—in order to better know their true identity.

This natural identity is a threat to the state; totalitarian regimes displace parents in pursuit of direct connection to the young precisely to cultivate a substitute identity, as with Mussolini's "Everything within the state, nothing outside the state, nothing against the state."[36] The family's natural obligations of loyalty compete against and conflict with the state's synthetic connections because they offer an identity that not only does not require the state but one that actually subverts it. Strong families mean a weak state and vice versa. And these relationships need not only be within a nuclear family; people can feel a kinship with others around the world as part of the shared human family—whether one views this through a religious lens as fellow children of God or simply as fellow secular travelers on the same tiny speck in a vast universe. This shared humanity is why the state must destroy identity before exercising its power; in war, soldiers are first conditioned to dehumanize the enemy, as "human beings need to find ways to overcome biological inhibitions against lethal aggression."[37] In other words, killing another person you view as your equal is difficult.

Nazi Germany was able to commit the atrocities that it did because the Jews were perceived by propagandized people as subhuman, stripped of their identity. Before the gas chambers came a methodical and deliberate campaign to make military officers—and the people at large—see Jews as vermin to be eradicated rather than people with family, friends, and feelings—like them. They were compelled to wear special insignia to mark them as an "other," separate from the rest of society. Jews were barred from public service so they would not be seen in any circumstance as being helpful to others. They were relocated to ghettos to create physical space away from the public where they could be persecuted and starved more easily. Jews were transported in cattle cars as a precursor to later being herded into gas chambers, conditioning soldiers to see the disheveled, sick, and worn people as mere animals to be prodded and put down, as necessary. And in the gas chambers, it was Zyklon-B that was used—a pesticide that was a fitting method of execution, perhaps, by a people who saw their victims as mere pests. Of course, this tactic is not reserved for the worst of the worst; it has also been employed emphatically by the "land of the free"—for example, when American soldiers barbarically tortured individuals at Guantanamo Bay and Abu Ghraib. "We were pretty much told that they were nobodies, that they were just enemy combatants," one participating soldier said. "I think that giving them the distinction of soldier would have changed our attitudes toward them."[38]

Families should feel threatened by the state's jealous eye toward its identity—and not merely because of militarist propaganda and other extreme examples. The family unit itself is a social bond that the state is all too willing to disrupt, even in the course of traditional parenting. Some judges, for example, assert that "there is no free-standing fundamental right of parents 'to control the upbringing of their children... in accordance with their personal and religious values and beliefs.'"[39] The U.S. Supreme Court once similarly proclaimed that "the state has a wide range of power for limiting parental freedom and authority in things affecting the child's welfare."[40] These legal rulings are buttressed by academics and attorneys, as in the case of one outspoken Harvard law professor who argued for a "presumptive ban"[41] on parents educating their own children, suggesting that "some homeschooling parents are extreme religious ideologues who . . . hold views in serious conflict with those generally deemed central in our society."[42] She continued:

> A very large proportion of homeschooling parents are ideologically committed to isolating their children from the majority culture and indoctrinating them in views and values that are in serious conflict with that culture.[43]

Others assert that parents have "no natural right to control their education fully,"[44] and that the state's role in education "has served as a check on the power of parents, and this is another powerful reason for maintaining it."[45] And true enough, there are bad parents; cases exist in which a child is being abused or neglected and needs outside support. Threads that otherwise would form a tight tapestry can be isolated and thus disconnected from its broader identity; plenty of stories highlight how some family connections are more chaotic than stable, and in these cases, the state is often embraced as a support system—a rescuer of last resort, helping those in need and providing a social safety net to give these children a leg up in life. But despite some justifiable cases, the state overall is not an innocent respondent to consequences but rather a contributor to them. It claims to resolve existing harms while creating many more of them. For example, government welfare programs purporting to support low-income families and needy children instead breed intergenerational dependence, suppress initiative, incentivize illegitimacy, and stifle intellectual development.[46] Some welfare programs have actively discouraged marriage because "welfare assistance went to mothers so long as no male was boarding in the household… Marriage to an employed male, even one earning the minimum wage, placed at risk a mother's economic well-being."[47] What are the long-term social impacts on children, and the corresponding growth of the state, in such an environment? Entire generations of children now grow up seeing the state as their savior, crediting to it their care and concern, at least in part. These powerful financial incentives took the rate of children being born out of wedlock from only 7 percent in 1964 to 40 percent today[48]—depriving many children of the "economically and politically independent family" they need to receive adequate nurturing and become a strong, independent adult. Many mothers have chosen cash over a companion, and the state has been all too eager to assist; according to one study, almost a third of Americans said they know someone who chose not to marry for fear of losing financial support from the state.[49]

The social bonds of family life provide strength and context to children who learn about them. These forces hold at bay the ever-present promises of the state to "help," for as government intervention increases, family ties weaken. Alexis de Tocqueville noticed the trend two centuries ago, observing that in past times "man almost always knows about his ancestors and respects them; his imagination extends to his great-grandchildren and he loves them." In other words, intergenerational loyalties and support were part of one's focus and feelings; individuals contemplated the long-term impact of their actions on family members. In contrast, de Tocqueville noticed even in his own day that "the duties of each to all are much clearer but devoted service to any individual much rarer. The bonds of human affection are wider but more relaxed… they form the habit of thinking of themselves in isolation."[50] Just as strong chains of molecules can be weakened by outside forces such that they become atomized, children can be isolated from their family, their social nakedness making them vulnerable to the influences and incentives they encounter. Parents who procreate but then invite the state as a co-provider and suitable support system for their children are relegating themselves to a primarily biological role wherein they effectively supply the state with fresh candidates to be shaped into submissive and supportive citizens. Only too late will these parents wake up and realize that the strong social forces that have captivated their children were welcomed earlier by them with open arms.

SPIRITUAL NAKEDNESS

Humans have an innate desire to understand life's most powerful questions. Who am I? Where did I come from? Where am I going? Is this life the end of my existence? The spiritual quest to understand one's self is deeply rooted, and rightly so—understanding the purpose of life gives it more meaning. And just as our social identity helps us give context to children about the connections they have and the strength they offer, our spiritual knowledge and beliefs add another layer of identity that helps families find meaning, purpose, and community. A person who believes in God and sees themselves as His child recognizes that they are a brother or sister to all of humanity; we all share this spiritual background and identity, which ideally unites us by cultivating feelings of love and charity toward others.

The state does not see the world this way. Its supposed omnipotence requires division, not unity; its identity is based on borders and separating its citizens from others. It is a tribalistic institution that needs enemies in order to thrive; it builds itself up by tearing others down—even those within its own ranks. Accordingly, authoritarian regimes of varying degrees perceive religion either as a threat or a tool. To minimize the threat, the state positions itself as a competing, counterfeit religion. And to use religion as a tool, the state co-opts people's spiritual feelings and beliefs to suit its purposes. Let's explore each approach in more detail.

Religion is a threat to the state because it holds God as a higher authority; God's law becomes superior to that of the secular state. And this is something that elected officials and despotic dictators alike struggle to tolerate. For example, early Christians who proclaimed Jesus as their Savior were seen by Caesar as traitors for suggesting such revolutionary tendencies that acknowledged a higher authority than the emperor, who considered himself a deity. One Roman soldier, Marcellus, was beheaded after declaring to his peers that he served "Jesus Christ the eternal King" and that he would "no longer serve your emperors."[51] His fate was shared by countless others who confessed Christ over Caesar. Dietrich Bonhoeffer affirmed his faith which required he condemn the horrendous actions of the Nazi regime, which responded by banning his books and hanging him for refusing to bend the knee. Even in the "land of the free," the state has long resisted religion's claim of moral superiority. "Can a man excuse his practices... because of his religious belief?" the U.S. Supreme Court wrote in *Reynolds v. United States*. "To permit this would be to make the professed doctrines of religious belief superior to the law of the land."[52] In a contest of authority, the Caesars of our day see religion as a threat to their claims of omnipotence. But not all threats are best dealt with in a frontal assault; sometimes, the most effective way to neutralize a threat is to adopt its tactics and traits—the "wolf in sheep's clothing" strategy. In this way, the state becomes a quasi-religious system itself—a replicated religion, if it can be called that, built for worshiping Caesar's might and cultivating loyalty to the tribe. Political temples and monuments (e.g., the Capitol, statues, Washington Monument) are erected for visitation and veneration. Rituals are created (e.g., voting, swearing into office) to encourage a shared political faith. Seminaries of learning (e.g., public schools and universities) ensure the rising generation learns what the state approves. Common prayers and hymns (e.g., the Pledge of Allegiance, the national anthem) cultivate fidelity and reverence. Sacred symbols and texts (e.g., the flag, the Constitution) are propagated to remind citizens of the state's greatness and presence—a shared identity for the masses. Like all great counterfeits, many people perceive these substitutions as legitimate and worthy of their devotion and support. "Abraham Lincoln used to say," remarked Rudy Giuliani, "that the test of your Americanism was... how much you believed in America. Because we're like a religion, really. A secular religion."[53] Secular societies find spiritual satisfaction in the state, seeing it as their savior of sorts. It scratches the innate itch for community, identity, and purpose without trifling with theological troubles. Consider the generational impacts of a society in which children perceive the state as the benevolent provider of food, education, housing, security, health care, and more; what need is there for God if the government can be counted on to attend to your every need?

Perhaps the rise of the state, and its subsequent acceleration of secularism by offering a counterfeit religion of sorts, is a causal factor in the marked decline in (traditional) religious observance and belief in recent decades. But despite this trend, plenty of people still seek spiritual meaning outside of the secular state; counterfeits don't satisfy everyone. For those who affirm a belief in God, the state stands ready to adopt the divine mantle for its rulers—redirecting people's religious attitudes to obey and acknowledge the authority of Caesar. Of course, mortal men proclaiming themselves as gods is nothing new. Political rulers have long asserted a claim to divine approbation and appointment. Egyptian pharaohs, Japanese emperors, Roman rulers, English kings, and modern-day rulers have all either claimed to be deity or claimed to have deity's support for their actions. Political rulers tend to appeal to and appear to appease the god or gods of the masses, leveraging people's religious feelings in support of the state's desired policies. By portraying himself a servant of God, Caesar can discourage dissent by encouraging the faithful to support his policies since he shares their faith. Religious texts are also interpreted to service the state's goals, as in the case of Romans 13 in the Bible, which some assert requires Christians to unquestioningly support the state, for "even a tyrant enjoyed divinely ordained authority and was owed the same loyalty and obedience as a good prince."[54] Colonists loyal to the Crown cheered on the many clergy who preached submission and argued against revolution, for "if even the most vile tyrants like Nero deserved obedience, how could it be just to resist George III?"[55] During the debate over slavery, some argued that scripture gave the practice "divine sanction"[56] partly because of the existing laws condoning it and the supposed obligation to support the state and its functionaries. As Hitler rose to power, churches were pressured to bend the knee and adorn their walls with Nazi banners and flags; pastors often reminded worshippers about their obligation to obey authority.[57] More recently, this co-opting of religious belief and claim of divine approval was cited during the U.S. government's forceful separation of parents and children crossing into the country's southern border. The Attorney General, Jeff Sessions, defended the policy separating children: "I would cite you to the Apostle Paul and his clear and wise command in Romans 13, to obey the laws of the government because God has ordained them for the purpose of order," he insufferably said. "Orderly and lawful processes are good in themselves and protect the weak and lawful."[58] The state wraps itself in the cloak of religion to ensure its subjects are supportive and submissive.

It is hard for the "naked individual"—and especially a child— to recognize and resist these trends. People's emotions are easily exploited by those who wish to gain power over them, whether they be individual abusers or authoritarians aiming to mold the masses. As the popular propagandist Edward Bernays once shockingly wrote, "We are governed, our minds are molded, our tastes formed, our ideas suggested, largely by men we have never heard of... In almost every act of our daily lives, whether... in our social conduct or our ethical thinking, we are dominated by the relatively small number of persons... who understand the mental processes and social patterns of the masses. It is they who pull the wires which control the public mind."[59] How can an adult, let alone a child, recognize the subtle emotional manipulations that inevitably shape our spiritual sentiments? It seems an extremely difficult proposition, for history clearly shows that for every Bonhoeffer resisting the state's spiritual intermeddling, the masses eagerly embrace it. This is nakedness at its core—an inability to shield yourself from exposure to psychological assault. The end result is a sort of "gulag of the mind,"[60] wherein people are emotionally incarcerated, trapped by the constraints imposed by thought controllers of a sort.

As prevalent as this situation is, however, it falls short of explaining the degree to which spiritual nakedness gives rise to the omnipotent state, whose external influences are formidable but not nearly as effective as the weakening of one's internal controls. Consider the widely held Judeo-Christian belief, popularized in the Protestant tradition in America's early colonial years, that a future judgment awaits us all and should therefore guide—and, where necessary, restrain—our actions in the present. This self-moderating spirituality tempered "the flesh" and shaped one's daily conduct. Philosophers and theologians alike pointed to the "future state of rewards and punishments"[61] as a basis for maintaining moral behavior in the present. The anticipation of a future day of rendered judgment can help conform one's actions to a social ideal that aims to improve not only his or her life but that of others as well—yet what happens when this spiritual standard is weakened or altogether absent? Recall that de Tocqueville observed that the state seeks to keep men "in perpetual childhood";[62] a person who does not mature or engage in so-called "adulting" is unwilling (or perhaps unable) to care for him or herself, let alone others. We consequently live in a society of juvenile dependents, eager to shirk their responsibility and myopically focus only on their instant gratifications. And what becomes the aggregate result of people looking to their present as opposed to a far-off, even eternal future? "The lack of internal control by individuals breeds external control by governments,"[63] offering the state yet another avenue to expand. Spiritual apathy prompts a hedonistic myopia that shirks responsibility and demands that others—and eventually an eager state, looking to expand its authority and influence—care for us and others in need.

In late December 2011, the state-approved television channel in North Korea broadcast footage of countless people wailing and crying over the death of Kim Jong-il, the country's "supreme leader." The world looked on in confused horror, wondering how such an oppressed people could feel sad for such a ruthless ruler. Were these crocodile tears, or was any part of it sincere? Was this an example of propaganda and brainwashing, or did North Koreans really reverence their leader enough to feel such emotion at his passing? The answer to each question might be an affirmative, to say nothing of the added expectation of performing in public, and the reality that those deemed insufficiently inconsolable might be incarcerated or worse. But the odd spectacle offers an extreme example of a spiritually naked people—boys and girls indoctrinated into an identity that ignores their individuality and elevates the collective above all; an atheistic culture that aggressively bans religious behavior that can "harm the state";[64] and the pervasive emotional influence the state can have over people who have every reason to hate its power and control. Despotic dictatorships should offer plenty of warnings for those living even in respectable republics since the spiritual selves of the rising generation are under assault from the competing Caesars of our day.

INTELLECTUAL NAKEDNESS

Yeonmi Park only ever knew the depressing enslavement of the brutal regime in North Korea. Born in 1993, she and her family grew up in a modern totalitarian state; Yeonmi was told from a young age that Americans were evil bastards. Children like her are paraded through museums enshrining the state's anti-Americanism, such as the "Sinchon Museum of American War Atrocities."[65] There they learn the horrors of the United States' actions against the North Korean people; this narrative is a current that runs deeply through the people's psyche due to constant conditioning from a young age. When Yeonmi finally fled with some close family at age fourteen, she found herself in South Korea—a nearby country but a different world that seemed far, far away from home. "It was very difficult to be free," she once said in an interview. "Everything [in North Korea] was decided for me. The government told me what to wear, what to listen to, what to watch. And suddenly in South Korea, they said 'what do you think?' And I was wondering, why does it matter what I think? Just tell me what to do."[66]

Hannah Arendt, a historian and researcher on totalitarianism, once wrote that the ideal subject for those who wish to rule is "people for whom the distinction between fact and fiction… no longer resist."[67] Yeonmi was taught from infancy an alternative reality about America, just as countless children throughout world history have been propagandized by the state to believe a certain set of "facts" that are partially or completely untrue. (The United States of America, of course, is not immune from this trend.) Compliant "journalists," if they can even be called by that title anymore, carry water for those in power and perpetuate a narrative that serves an agenda rather than the cause of truth. Entire systems are built around the desire to persuade people that the emperor is wearing clothes when those who rely on their own faculties would clearly see that he is, in fact, naked.

But it is our nakedness that the state wants—and perhaps in no other area of our lives do we see this play out more than with our minds. What Bernays referred to as "an invisible government" and the "conscious and intelligent manipulation"[68] of people—so-called "choice architects"[69] in Sunstein's language—is the intentional engineering of consent to preserve and augment political power for those at the top. And that consent matters, for as the Declaration of Independence states, it's how governments ultimately operate; without it, the people tend to rise up against their rulers. And while *informed, explicit* consent is the only kind that matters, the state knows that people will tolerate implied consent based on limited information. In short, the government can get away with a lot—classifying its troubling activities and depriving its citizens of access to information that might lead them to revolt. Truth is treason, as they say, in an empire of lies.

The Korean War came to a close on July 27, 1953—creating a new North Korea that consigned children like Yeonmi to its propaganda-laden totalitarianism. Just a few weeks prior, Allen Dulles rose to the podium to deliver prepared remarks to the assembled alumni of Princeton University at a conference in Hot Springs, Virginia. As the first civilian director of the Central Intelligence Agency, appointed just two months prior to the speech, Dulles focused his speech on what he called "brain warfare" and "brain perversion techniques" being perpetrated by the Soviets:

> Its aim is to condition the mind so that it no longer reacts on a free will or rational basis but responds to impulses implanted from outside.

If we are to counter this kind of warfare we must understand the techniques the Soviet is adopting to control men's minds…

The human mind is the most delicate of all instruments. It is so finely adjusted, so susceptible to the impact of outside influences that it is proving a malleable tool in the hands of sinister men… We in the West are somewhat handicapped in brain warfare.[70]

Dulles further claimed that "it is hard for us to realize that in the great area behind the Iron Curtain a vast experiment is underway to change men's minds, working on them continuously from youth to old age."[71] But what Dulles never shared in his remarks is that efforts were already underway by the CIA, overseen and approved by him personally, to experiment with mind control at levels that would dwarf anything being done by the Soviets. What Dulles deceptively decried as "abhorrent to our way of life" was literally being implemented under his order, issued three days after his speech. Known as Project MKUltra, this top-secret program involved mind control experiments using electro-shock therapy, drugs, toxins, hypnosis, radiation, and more. Some participants had volunteered freely for the program; most were enrolled under coercion or without any knowledge that they were human guinea pigs for the CIA's activities. Soldiers, prisoners, mentally impaired individuals, and other vulnerable members of society were lab rats for Dulles' project. While governments had long sought to engineer consent through changing popular opinion, now some were turning to weaponizing science and psychology to coerce consent by reengineering the human brain. What North Korea did to Yeonmi Park was horrible. What the United States of America did was far worse. Program managers had concluded that "unwitting [participants] would be desirable"[72]—and compounding the immorality of experimenting on the unknowing was the secrecy of the whole affair, encouraged even by those in an oversight role, such as the CIA's Inspector General, four years later:

Precautions must be taken not only to protect operations from exposure to enemy forces but also to conceal these activities from the American public in general. The knowledge that the Agency is engaging in unethical and illicit activities would have serious repercussions in political and diplomatic circles and would be detrimental to the accomplishment of its mission.[73]

Dulles had warned that others' efforts to control men's minds have "such far reaching implications that it is high time for us to realize what it means and the problems it presents in thwarting our own program for spreading the gospel of freedom."[74] But does the state truly care about our freedom? One might argue that this "gospel" was nothing more than a façade to mask the state's true intentions—the preservation of power and control of others. Its activities involved infringing upon the freedom of non-consenting individuals. And contrary to what some might claim—such as President George W. Bush announcing he had "abandoned free market principles to save the free market system" by pumping trillions of dollars into the economy—you can't support a value by violating it. Just as moral governance requires informed consent, the omnipotent state prefers ignorance—intellectual nakedness—to get away with its misdeeds. And so, it's not surprising that years later, as prying eyes started asking questions, Project MKUltra's director told subordinates that "it would be a good idea if [the MKUltra] files were destroyed."[75] Thus, many of the details of one of the government's most unethical undertakings were scrubbed from history.

The control of others' minds need not be so insidious or expansive. Indeed, the human brain is predisposed to trusting others.[76] Within a few hours of birth, an infant is already looking into the eyes of his mother and turning his head in the direction of her voice.[77] Children mimic their parents and (largely) follow their instructions. These natural authority figures guide the young through their most formative years until their brains have further developed into decision-making engines that can help them chart their own course. But adults can be as intellectually naked as their immature offspring; the development of one's prefrontal cortex doesn't guarantee it will be used well. Trust in and deference to authority, over even one's own conscience, has been consistently demonstrated in psychological studies, as in the case of the infamous Milgram experiment in which two-thirds of adults were willing to administer potentially lethal shocks of electricity to a stranger when an apparent authority dressed in an official-looking laboratory coat ordered them to do so.[78] Without evidence, people often believe and do what they are told—whether it's believing that Saddam Hussein was somehow involved in the 9/11 attacks,[79] taking FDA-approved drugs that caused countless deaths,[80] or distorting their diet based on the politically-controlled and scientifically-problematic food pyramid pushed on schoolchildren and their families for decades.[81] The boy keeps crying wolf, but people keep listening to him.

Yeonmi's experience, tragic as it was, is not totally dissimilar from that of a child in the so-called "land of the free" she was taught to hate. School curriculum regularly inculcates into children's minds the narrative preferred by those in power, omitting details that the state finds unflattering. Textbooks tell tales of past wars that glorify the state's successes and downplay or disregard its failures. Government schools exclude from their materials anything that erodes confidence in and support for the government, such as Project MKUltra. And myths are routinely taught as truths—leading children to unquestioningly believe that Abraham Lincoln wanted to free slaves, that the New Deal stopped the depression, or that spreading democracy abroad is a noble and appropriate goal for the federal government. Of course, children don't know any better— and even as adults, many have not been exposed to contrary ideas (and actual truth) that would dispel the deep programming they were exposed to when they were young. Even when the truth is easily available, as in the lie about Saddam previously mentioned, people continue to believe what they were first told by those in authority; a poll conducted five years after the 9/11 attack found that 43 percent of Americans still believed Saddam was personally involved.[82] Some people, it seems, prefer to remain intellectually naked.

And why does the state want us to be this way? The answer was shared by Horace Mann, who first institutionalized modern schooling in Massachusetts in 1837. "Men are cast-iron," he said, "but children are wax."[83] Consent is more easily engineered[84] with the raw materials of an empty, impressionable mind. And it is through children that the state can oppose the dissenting political views of their parents, as exemplified by Hitler's dismissive retort to opponents that "in a short time, [their children would] know nothing else but this new community."[85] Young minds are fertile soil for the seeds of statist propaganda. This is why since Horace Mann's day, the state has taken particular interest in "public" education—government-run schools to shape the minds of the young. John Dewey, a socialist pioneer of modern schooling, said in 1928 that he loved that schools had a rule "in building up forces… whose natural effect is to undermine the importance and uniqueness of family life."[86] On another occasion, he observed proudly that "the increase of importance of public schools has been at least coincident with the relaxation of older ties."[87] Families that propagate and preserve their values are an obstacle to central planners and collectivists like Mann, Dewey, and their pedagogical progeny today. Indeed, the state's classrooms have "become a place where intense psychological warfare is being waged against all traditional values."[88]

Those who don't learn from the past are doomed to repeat it, so politicians prefer that people not be aware of past problems. Historical ignorance is a scholastic imperative for the state. Civic illiteracy is bemoaned by many but cheered on by those in control. Mencken was right to note that the state desires "to breed and train a standardized citizenry, to put down dissent and originality."[89] Predictability is preferred to the chaotic independence of free, informed people. Government schools all but guarantee this result, having dumbed down generations of individuals into a malleable mass of mediocrity.[90] If "war is the health of the state,"[91] then a state-run schooling system is its lifeblood. Without it, statism is impossible. With it, the state becomes inevitable.

FAMILY INDEPENDENCE

"The essential psychological characteristic of our age is the predominance of fear over self-confidence... Everyone of every class tries to rest his individual existence on the bosom of the state and tends to regard the state as the universal provider."[1]

—Bertrand de Jouvenel

BETWEEN THE OMNIPOTENT STATE and the naked individual lies the natural family—the "only thing that the free man makes for himself and by himself,"[2] in the words of G. K. Chesterton—which Novak suggests offers the first line of resistance to protect against totalitarian tendencies. This natural and inherently localizing organization of mankind is one with which we are all familiar. But what is it about this institution that is so critical in protecting naked individuals from the omnipotent state? Why must families be independent in order to resist? And what does that independence look like?

Independent families have the authority and autonomy to "raise, manage, train, educate, provide for, and reasonably discipline"[3] their children; the state's role, if any, must be "secondary and supportive to the primary role of a parent."[4] And yet, this pattern is the exception rather than the norm. The Wunderlich family knows this tragedy all too well. On August 29, 2013, Dirk Wunderlich saw thirty-three armed police officers approaching his home, saying they wanted to enter and speak with him. "I tried to ask questions," Dirk said, "but within seconds, three police officers brought a battering ram and were about to break the door in, so I opened it."[5] Officers forced Dirk to remain seated in a chair and not make a phone call. They informed him they had a court order to remove his children from the home. One might presume that such an order was issued based on allegations of abuse or neglect. Not so in this case: Dirk and his wife Petra were accused of homeschooling.

The Wunderlichs were not permitted to speak to their crying children before they were carried away, nor were they told where the children would be relocated. "When my wife tried to give my daughter a kiss and a hug goodbye," Dirk described, "one of the special agents roughly elbowed her out of the way and said – 'It's too late for that.' What kind of government acts like this?"[6] As any good parents would, Dirk and Petra fought for their natural rights to educate their children and get them back. When the children were later returned, they were ordered by the state to attend government school. And it was that very schooling authority that contested the Wunderlich's court battle to homeschool their children. One official—despite never having visited the family's home nor speaking with the children—wrote to the court that "I am certainly of the opinion that there is a danger to the children, because they are systematically withdrawn from all social aspects of society and live in a so-called parallel society."[7] After several years of court battles to defend their right to educate their children, the Wunderlichs lost; the European Court of Human Rights ruled that the family had not "provided sufficient evidence that the children were properly educated and socialized."[8] The court further held that the state has "a duty to protect children" due to "reasonably held concerns"[9] and thus upheld Germany's prohibition on homeschooling—a law on the books since 1938, when the Nazis passed the *Reichsschulpflichtgesetz* (Law on Compulsory Education in the German Reich) which, in its very first section, begins with this:

> **Compulsory general education.** In the German Reich there is compulsory education. It secures the education and instruction of German youth in the spirit of National Socialism. It is subject to all children and adolescents of German nationality who are domiciled or habitually resident in the country. Compulsory education must be fulfilled by attending a German school. Exceptions are decided by the school inspectorate.[10]

The Nazi view on parents teaching their own children was that such behavior was anti-nationalistic and opposed to the state's identity and goals to create loyal, submissive citizens. And while exceptions were provided for, none are allowed today "for pedagogical or religious reasons."[11] Indeed, it was the view of the European court in a previous homeschooling case that education "by its very nature calls for regulation by the state."[12] Families are thus forced to be dependent upon the state—and not only in Germany. Until the 1980s, home education was banned throughout almost all of the "land of the free," with only three states allowing it.[13] Parents were regularly fined, arrested, and their children removed and placed in foster care.

It's ironic when families are forced into dependence upon the state because the state is dependent upon families. The rising generation is the support pipeline for the state, providing a steady stream of taxpaying rule followers to create a society in the state's image. Perpetuating its power and programs is why the state is so often obsessed with the population replacement rate, in some cases incentivizing women to have children through cash bonuses, as happens in Russia,[14] Australia,[15] Estonia,[16] and many more countries;[17] governments around the world have, crazy as it sounds, "started paying for babies."[18] This perverse parasitic relationship requires the state to present itself as a help to families rather than a hinderance, masking its intentions and effects. Falling into this trap, families become dependent upon the state without understanding the implications of the relationship and consequently expose their children—and future generations—to a slow decay of autonomy, freedom, and integrity. Dependent families are compromised families.

Such dependence is especially problematic because it teaches children the wrong message about how individuals should behave and associate with others. Instead of being taught to respect and leave alone the property of others, they are taught that such items are subject only to their desires and that all they need is a majority of people to side with them to take it for themselves. Instead of acting, they are acted upon—at the mercy of external circumstances not of their making, to be bailed out by others for any bad decisions or mistakes they make. Instead of self-reliance, they are encouraged to avail themselves of so-called social safety nets woven together from the stolen goods of others. Instead of objective truth, they are taught to speak "their" truth, and that morality is subjective. Instead of thinking critically and speaking out against abuse and wrongdoing, they are taught not to bite the hands that feed them. Thoreau once allegedly said that "Disobedience is the true foundation of liberty. The obedient must be slaves."[19] Dependent families dare not question the state, for they are at its mercy and thrive only with its support. They are willing slaves, falsely thinking they are free.

Despite ample historical examples in which families either willingly or reluctantly come to depend upon the state, it is the institution of the family that has long outlived the rise and fall of countless authoritarian regimes. Nations have come and gone, but the family remains. It is this entity that has always nurtured the individual, instilling virtues and values that are integral to freedom: personal responsibility, honesty, hard work, and moral agency. And these "traditions of the fathers" are the cumulative influence of generations long before—the "democracy of the dead," as G.K. Chesterton called it[20]—which offers families the collected wisdom that resists submission "to the small and arrogant oligarchy of those who merely happen to be walking about."[21] This knowledge and tradition are not taught in textbooks; the state's schools do not teach the dangers of the state. The values nurtured by the family can't be imposed in top-down fashion, for they typically conflict with the whims of the controlling few and their "fatal conceit"[22] that the state's functionaries possess the knowledge and skill to control the actions and outcomes of the masses. Culture is cultivated, not inculcated.

Where the state centralizes power, the institution of the family is a decentralizing counteragent. The distribution of humankind into tiny tribes, each with their own experiences, traditions, perspectives, and goals, creates a political terrain full of barriers the state must overcome to succeed. And the state succeeds best not by running roughshod over these many barriers but by persuading families to remove them themselves.

Imagine a homeowner whose neighbor begins spreading his possessions across her front lawn. The neighbor continues this process until it appears to the homeowner that he has crossed her property line, his items now occupying part of her front lawn. But she is actually not that certain about where the property line actually exists; and the neighbor's strong personality, coupled with his insistence that he has done no wrong, induces her to put up with the encroachment. Her ignorance inhibits her independence; she cannot assert rights she is uncertain about. This predicament faces many families who, as the "first line of resistance against totalitarianism," fail to discharge their duty because dependence is familiar and convenient—they are ignorant as to how families might be economically and politically independent and why that is so crucial to preserve their freedom and keep the state at bay.

What would such a family look like?

ECONOMIC INDEPENDENCE

Benjamin Franklin spent around two decades in England, just prior to the launch of the American Revolution, as a sort of ambassador for various colonial interests. He was thrust into the middle of many political conflicts and debates, including one that had been raging for years: how to care for the poor. For nearly two centuries, the Crown had been imposing a coercive wealth redistribution system to generate welfare funds and mandate the provision of labor to the poor who needed it. But in Franklin's day, the system's growth was accelerating substantially; in the first half of the eighteenth century, nominal welfare expenditures increased by 72 percent "despite the fact that prices were falling and population was growing slowly."[23] In other words, England's welfare state was growing when it should have been shrinking.

Franklin wore many hats, including that of an economist. He understood how incentives operate, and he had observed in other countries that when "more public provisions were made for the poor, the less they provided for themselves, and of course became poorer."[24] Conversely, "the less that was done for them, the more they did for themselves, and became richer." He felt that "the best way of doing good to the poor, is not making them easy *in* poverty, but leading or driving them *out* of it." Ultimately, the incentive to live at the expense of others' labor is a tempting one that the state had institutionalized for decades:

> The day you passed [the welfare law in England], you took away from before their eyes the greatest of all inducements to industry, frugality, and sobriety, by giving them a dependence on somewhat else than a careful accumulation during youth and health, for support in age or sickness. In short, you offered a premium for the encouragement of idleness, and you should not now wonder that it has had its effect in the increase of poverty.[25]

Franklin was not a fortune teller, and England was not an exception; what he described about the situation in one country over two centuries ago is still relevant to ours today. The U.S., for example, is "on the verge of a symbolic threshold: the point at which more than half of all American households receive and accept [financial] benefits from the government."[26] In the past half a century, and after adjusting for income and population growth, entitlement payments to the supposedly poor grew by an astonishing 727 percent.[27] Behind the numbers are millions of people acting on incentives and changing their behavior based on what they might receive in return.

Peggy Joseph took her daughter out of school one Wednesday morning in 2008 to see a speech by Barack Obama, the then-presidential candidate. Following that speech, her emotions were running high as she spoke with a reporter. "It was the most memorable time of my life!" she proudly exclaimed. And then, the real reason for the excitement: "I won't have to worry about puttin' gas in my car, I won't have to worry about payin' my mortgage. If I help him [get elected], he's gonna help me."[28] Four years later, in Cleveland, one woman went viral for praising the incumbent for providing her a free phone.[29] "Keep Obama president!" she told her interviewer. "He gave us a phone. He's going to do more!"[30] When asked about the other leading candidate, all she could offer was, "He sucks, bad!" Presumably, her discontent was partly due to the perception that her government benefits, phone included, might not expand as generously under the other guy's leadership. Today, entire stadiums are filled for political events with people attracted by the promise of free health care, free tuition, free retirement benefits, and on and on. And despite the prevailing perception that the Democratic Party is primarily responsible for the state's heavy welfare spending, "entitlements were actually highest during Republican administrations. The political allure of *free* is bi-partisan."[31] Put differently, promising free things is an inherent function of the state apparatus itself, regardless of the partisan leanings of those who temporarily control it.

When the state subsidizes nearly half the population, the societal shift is palpable; America's past character of self-reliance and industry is being replaced with a new identity as a nation of takers. Families are increasingly embracing a relationship of dependence, with some parents trying to game the system to milk whatever benefits they can at the expense of others. This is not merely a symptom of weak families; it is a causal byproduct of broken families with increasing fatherlessness driving the dependence. Some welfare programs feature incentives that have "actively discouraged marriage" since "welfare assistance went to mothers so long as no male was boarding in the household…"[32] Half a century ago, only seven percent of American children were born out of wedlock. Today that number exceeds 40 percent.[33] Effectively, the government paid mothers to keep fathers out of the home—and these steep financial incentives forced a wedge into families to break them apart. Among families that include married parents, only 6.8 percent are dependent upon the state, but for single-parent, female-headed families, that number skyrockets to 37.1 percent.[34] Where traditionally fathers were providers, in broken families, the state becomes the provider; in some cases, women refuse the aid of a husband or the father of her children to remain dependent upon the state. Breadwinners are abandoned in favor of proverbial (and literal) breadlines.

The waste and failures of the modern welfare system are well known; we know what dependent families look like, and we have reviewed some of the dangers of such dependence. But what does an economically independent family look like? What ideals must we aspire to in order to keep the state at bay and provide children the necessary nurture they need?

- **Practice personal responsibility.** Economically independent families understand that they should not be a burden on others and are not entitled to others' labor and property. Parents have the burden and opportunity to demonstrate this to their children through their actions, for parents who preach but do not practice personal responsibility are unlikely to help their children learn its importance and live it themselves. Parents should set a realistic financial budget for the family based on their available and anticipated income; the family should live on less than it earns. Purchases should not be made that exceed what the family can pay; debt should be generally avoided unless it is strategically and prudently used by those who have the ability to pay it back. Failures and setbacks should not be blamed on others; parents should demonstrate to their children the importance of accepting the reality of their situation and determining a path forward to make the most of their circumstances, whatever they are. Support may be sought when needed, but such support should come from extended family, community, church, or other nongovernmental sources. Where possible, debts should be repaid or paid forward to benefit others, showing children the importance of developing the personal integrity that comes with not forcing others, through the state, to bear their family's burdens.

- **Reap what you sow.** Truly temporary assistance (a so-called "social safety net") may be tolerated, even from the state—yet what is thought of to be temporary often becomes long term and resistant to change. As Ronald Reagan once quipped, government programs are "the nearest thing to eternal life we'll ever see on this earth";[35] too often, the net entangles those whom it catches with its perverse economic incentives. Oddly, and perhaps hypocritically, the architect of some of these programs himself warned of their danger. President Franklin D. Roosevelt, patron saint of modern welfare programs for his New Deal, among other initiatives, once wrote that history clearly showed that "continued dependence upon relief induces a spiritual disintegration fundamentally destructive to the national fiber. To dole out relief in this way is to administer a narcotic, a subtle destroyer of the human spirit."[36] Economically independent families know that their actions are about more than merely money; how we manage our physical resources affects our mental and spiritual being. Reaping what we sow, instead of being dependent upon the production of others, allows us to avoid this "disintegration" while also placing ourselves in a position to support others who may be in need, creating a virtuous cycle where our thrift, savings, and hard work allow us to help others do the same.

- **Create value for others.** Economically independent families produce more than they consume. They identify opportunities to create multiple streams of income, so they are not reliant upon the good graces of one employer to heavily influence their financial fate. They are industrious problem solvers, offering their solutions to others—either as a charitable activity or as a way to earn money. Children are trained to see challenges as opportunities, thinking of entrepreneurial ways to solve problems in a win-win way that can benefit those they help as well as produce income to provide for themselves. They are also taught that political promises and programs are inefficient and counterproductive to solving problems; economically independent families see government as a threat to their survival—not a support. In all things, such families focus on creating value for those around them and being a positive force in the world, rather than a negative sum set of dependents upon others.

- **Act instead of being acted upon.** The state prefers people to play the role of victim, for whom it can then act as a savior; it desires to be seen as the solution to their problems. Thus, the state's propaganda arm, through the media and schools, foments victimhood and encourages minorities and the poor to see themselves as intrinsically oppressed, suffering from circumstances outside of their control. This cultivates a culture of dependency that keeps the citizenry sedated—a preferred position for a state that wishes to maintain and increase its control. Economically independent families recognize that they can influence their circumstances instead of being victims of them. They seek to positively influence the world around them, beginning with their own family; they act instead of merely being acted upon. Parents teach their children that there is more to life than subsistence and entertainment; one of the benefits of financial wealth is that it allows people to have time, energy, and resources that they can devote to other causes. Dependent people are narrowly focused on the hand-to-mouth daily maintenance of their lives, unable to positively influence the world around them; dependent people are slaves to the circumstances others create for them.

- **Divide labor.** Family operations involve a variety of tasks—cooking, cleaning, teaching, yard maintenance, pet care, income generation, appliance upkeep, and much more. Parents who want to raise independent and competent children recognize that these should be shared tasks as soon as possible. Children are given assignments ("chores") as part of supporting the family, which allows them to learn new skills, and have responsibilities with accountability for their performance. And while the division of labor leads to greater prosperity, prudent parents also ensure that their children become well rounded through exposure to a variety of tasks and knowledge, thus broadening their abilities as an adult—knowing how to change a tire, do taxes, meal plan, budget, and more. In effect, an economically independent family creates their own microcosm of the economy within their household with parents and children each serving and exchanging goods and services with one another. Children come to learn that they are expected to work hard to support the family and that negative consequences arise from their failure—in the process, understanding that their behavior impacts more people than just themselves.

- **Create family capital.** Economically independent families provide their children with resources to learn and practice economic independence themselves—financial, social, human, and more. Parents teach their children to reject attitudes of victimhood and dependence and instead to see problems as opportunities for entrepreneurial endeavors to help others. Parents teach their children how businesses operate and encourage them to practice this knowledge through applied learning, whether something as simple as a lemonade stand or a more serious microenterprise such as babysitting, lawn mowing, selling items online, or offering a service such as graphic design, translation, marketing, etc. And this family capital is clearly successful, for the likelihood that someone's business ventures will succeed increases by up to 27 percent if that person "worked in a family business prior to starting his or her own business."[37] Economic independence is as much about training children to have an entrepreneurial and productive mindset for future success as it is about parents pressing toward their own financial success in the short term.

As delegates to the Second Continental Congress deliberated during the spring and summer of 1776, significant threats were hanging over their heads should they have decided to move for independence. Affixing their signatures to the Declaration of Independence was a point of no return; either they were going to gain their freedom from England and "provide new guards for their future security," as the document said, or they were going to lose the war to the world's most powerful military, forfeit all of their possessions, ruin their families, and be hanged, drawn, and quartered.[38] With firm resolve, and despite the risk, they signed—but would this have happened if the eminent men participating in that process were poor and barely able to provide for their families after a full day's toil in the fields? If the individuals who comprised the founding generation were necessarily preoccupied with meeting their families' basic needs or depending on the support of others for their subsistence, they would not have had the free time, energy, and resources needed to be engaged in the revolutionary events that changed the course of history. Because of their economic independence, they were afforded the opportunity to pursue other interests. Had these specific individuals not had the financial wherewithal to be away from their homes for so long a period, who might have been sent in their place? Would other economically independent men have been as courageous and principled? One might conclude that the war for America's independence was predicated in part upon the economic independence of the founding statesmen. For our families, in like measure, our political independence is closely connected to our economic independence; we cannot adequately secure our freedom if we are financially dependent upon the state. As Thomas Paine once wrote, "Those who expect to reap the blessing of freedom, must, like men, undergo the fatigue of supporting it."[39] That support is most likely to come from those individuals who can afford the time and money necessary to make a significant and lasting impact. If we wish for freedom from the state, our families must be economically independent from it.

POLITICAL INDEPENDENCE

"The first time I couldn't buy food at the grocery store, I was 15 years old," wrote Daniel Di Martino, who grew up in Caracas, Venezuela. This was in 2014 and, after an hour of waiting in line, he realized that he had forgotten his government-issued identification card—without it, "the government rationing system would not let the supermarket sell my family the full quota of food we needed. It was four days until the government allowed me to buy more."[40]

Daniel tells how this was normal life for him, living under a socialist regime where the state was taking over various industries and sectors of the economy in an effort to make things less expensive or even free. Days or weeks would go by without water, and the government's nationalization of the electrical market led to rolling blackouts. Product shortages abounded. And, predictably, the central bank significantly inflated the currency—the state's hammer, leading every market problem to appear as a nail. "When Chavez took office in 1999," Daniel explained, "my parents were earning several thousand dollars a month between the two of them. By 2016, due to inflation, they earned less than $2 a day."[41]

Of course, Daniel's experience is not unique. Communist regimes, socialist states, and totalitarian dictatorships in world history have all produced massive suffering, starvation, and death—undermining the ability of families to care for themselves economically and destroying any pretense of political power they might have otherwise enjoyed. Millions of Russian peasants were dispossessed of their land and deported after the abolition of private ownership.[42] Tens of millions of Chinese residents were starved, beaten, and worked to death during Mao's "Great Leap Forward."[43] Countless millions in multiple countries endured a "carefully cultivated Auschwitz of the mind" under regimes pervaded with propaganda and concerted thought control.[44] Ignore for a moment the pervasive suffering, destruction, displacement, and misallocation of scarce resources causing families harm as a result of central planning of the economy and the exertion of political control over people's private affairs and personal decisions. Focusing on death alone, the number of people killed by their own government during the twentieth century is four times more than the number of people who died in combat or as so-called collateral damage during all the various foreign and internal wars.[45]

These horrendous scandals can be deceiving by diverting our attention entirely to them when discussing the political abuses of the omnipotent state. It would be incorrect and naive to assume that similar circumstances are not seen in democratic forms of government and modern states as well; tyranny lite is still not freedom. The suffering a family endures because of a state action might be tolerable in small amounts: a high tax rate preventing savings for retirement; a policy overregulating their profession, hindering business growth; a zoning law prohibiting the construction of a "mother-in-law" apartment to care for an elderly parent in the home; or an anti-gun law rendering a single mother defenseless against an armed intruder invading her home. Supposedly small violations of freedom are still significant to those who experience them, despite the ease with which they are ignored by those who wield the levers of power. And while it is more difficult to quantify the dispersed burdens imposed on the masses, they are no less real for those who suffer from their short- and long-term effects.

Family independence and the individual freedom it fosters cannot be achieved merely by accumulating wealth; economic independence alone is insufficient to keep the state at bay and nurture children into strong individuals who can exercise and defend their freedom. The full realization of family independence comes through political freedom—not just granted by a benevolent or limited government but asserted and ardently defended by those who embrace their role as protectors, providers, and primary caretakers of their children. A family that flexes its freedom is a threat to the state's power, which is why its programs and propaganda aim to undermine the strength and cohesion of the natural family. This control comes through central planning in top-down fashion, institutionalizing the *fatal conceit* that a few people in power know what's best for the many. F.A. Hayek once wrote that the "curious task of economics is to demonstrate to men how little they really know about what they imagine they can design."[46] And yet, despite an ample record of failure on the part of the state's functionaries and planners, it presses forward to "shape the world… according to [its] wishes."[47] This centralized remaking of society is necessarily at odds with the decentralized and spontaneous nature of autonomous families, each determining what is best for them. This is essentially totalitarianism—imposing a "single, central ordering philosophy" on the public by "subordinating everyone's individual plans and purposes to the static vision of a powerful elite."[48] Society will be arranged in some form or fashion; it's not a question of whether it will. The question we must face is how it will be arranged and by whose design. Will the few decide for the many, or will the many have the freedom to decide for themselves?

Parents interpose themselves between the omnipotent state and the "naked individuals" they conceive and rear to protect their literal creations from a destroying force. The state is good at many things, and nearly all of them relate to destruction; when you're a hammer, everything looks like a nail. Central planners wielding their concentrated political authority are experts in "pulverizing the delicate fabric of evolved civilized life,"[49] whether through drones and soldiers or sinister policies and evil economic incentives. The state can't create; that role belongs to society, each family a single thread that creates strength and beauty in the broader (but delicate) social fabric. Childbearing, language development, new businesses, mentorship, love, innovation, and more—the many acts of creation cultivate independence and individuality, which the state cannot abide. But politically independent families know the stakes and proceed anyway. They don't need the state, don't want the state, and see it as their primary obstacle toward prosperity and peace.

The destructive activities of the state are well known; we know what happens to families when their basic freedoms are undermined by totalitarian regimes. But what does a politically independent family look like? What ideals must we aspire to in order to keep the state at bay and provide children the necessary nurture they need?

- **Cultivate critical thinking.** Adolf Eichmann was a major player in perpetrating the Holocaust of the Jews, directly overseeing the logistics required to deport millions of Jewish men, women, and children to ghettos and extermination camps. After the war, he was able to flee to Argentina using false papers, where he was kidnapped by Israeli agents in 1960, relocated to Israel, and charged with war crimes and crimes against humanity. His trial was widely televised, in part to educate the public about the crimes committed against Jews. One of the many people who watched the trial unfold was Stanley Milgram, a social psychologist at Yale, who wondered whether Eichmann's defense—that he was "just following orders," as it were—could explain why his many accomplices, and the German people more broadly, went along with what they were told to do. Just three months after the Eichmann trial began, Milgram launched his previously mentioned experiment, in which participants were instructed to perform an act that violated their conscience: the administration of a series of electric shocks upon a person in another room whom they could hear but not see. Each shock, participants were told, would be more powerful and painful than the last, leading to a final, fatal voltage being delivered. Of course, no pain was actually inflicted upon the unseen person, but participants did not know this and could only hear the unseen person's screams of agony. As participants protested throughout the process, they were instructed by the authority figure to continue— that the experiment was important and required completion. Reluctantly, but compliantly, most participants subordinated their concerns and did as instructed, to the point of (in their minds) administering death to another. The Milgram experiment has been consistently replicated, with results showing that over 60 percent of participants will inflict the fatal voltage upon the other person when instructed to do so by the authority figure.[50] This frightening trend should terrify families who wish to raise children who are independent and value truth and morality, even (and especially) when pressured by someone to reject it. It suggests that we must be intentional in our efforts to empower our children to understand what is right and be willing to defend it—even against those who are perceived to be in power. In this manner, critical thinking is more about skepticism of what others claim or instruct than it is about simply asking questions, as it is commonly perceived. While the "habits and opinions of the masses" are often molded by those in power through "conscious and intelligent manipulation,"[51] as Bernays wrote, politically independent families recognize and reject this trend by encouraging their children to evaluate each action and idea on its merits, regardless of the supposed authority figure decreeing or defending it. In short, political independence requires an intellectual stubbornness in the pursuit and defense of truth.

- **Debate and discuss important issues.** Why might people be so prone to deferring to authority, even to the point of killing someone? How has the state been able to captivate and control countless millions to do its destructive bidding, even going against their own personal interests? Perhaps part of the answer is the way children are raised to perceive and respond to authority figures—and parents are the first and foremost authorities in a child's life. If we present ourselves to our children as omnipotent or omniscient (or omnipresent, as some overbearing mothers might like to suggest...), then we deprive our children of the necessary nuance to see that even we, their parents, are fallible, sometimes biased, and often ignorant. Though parents possess a natural and appropriate authority, this can be abused if children are led to believe that they must believe and act as their parents do. Our children should be able to challenge us, and we should admit when we are wrong. They should see us as fellow students, seeking knowledge alongside them. Fostering family discussions is a fantastic way to let our children formulate and explore independent ideas and entertain arguments that oppose ours. In a safe setting around the proverbial dinner table, we can raise the topics of the day or ideas from the past and provide opportunities to expand critical thinking skills through vigorous discussion. One of the most important reasons for fostering discussion of this sort is to allow children to advance their own arguments on the basis of knowledge and reason instead of regurgitating what they were told by their parents, teachers, or another authority figure. After all, someone who defends an idea by appealing to authority is not using their own intelligence; they are simply using their memory.

- **Learn from history, not about it.** Growing up in Romania in the late 1970s, Carmen Alexe can recall the occasions when her mother would wake up at 2 a.m. to go to the store, four hours before it opened, to stand in line in hopes of being able to purchase milk, butter, eggs, and yogurt during the rare times they were available. Soon after, the totalitarian regime, attempting to centrally plan the Romanian economy, implemented food rationing. Carmen's family of four was allowed one kilogram of flour and one kilogram of sugar per month—if such products were even available, which was not always the case.[52] Now, living in the United States, Carmen—and countless immigrants like her from former Soviet states—watches in shock and dismay as the "land of the free" embraces many of the ideologies and attitudes that led to the economic deprivation and loss of freedom experienced in their former homelands. This trend toward supporting the state is largely because young people do not understand its true nature and record of evil depravity. Shockingly, only 57 percent of millennials believe the Declaration of Independence better guarantees freedom and quality over *The Communist Manifesto*. Seventy percent of them would vote for a socialist.[53] Politically independent families understand that their children need to be informed about the reality of the state and the history of its many atrocities. They know that not repeating past mistakes requires

learning about them. And they realize that the state's schools—
and its teachers and textbooks—are not going to dispassionately
and fairly provide this information. At best, history education
in modern schools teaches children *about* the past as if they are
walking through a museum full of curiosities and anachronistic
relics of a bygone era not relevant to their advanced, present-day
lives. But this superficial review of history is insufficient to fully
understand *why* things happened in the past and how similar ideas
are present today, even if the packaging has been updated. Just
as a well-traveled person is not likely to be "deceived by the local
errors of his native village," C. S. Lewis once said, a student of
history "has lived in many times and is therefore in some degree
immune from the great cataract of nonsense that pours from the
press and the microphone of his own age."[54] Those who value
freedom must learn from history who its chief opponent is and
how it operates in our day.

- **Create traditions together.** The omnipotent state thrives when
its subjects are socially atomized and historically ignorant. Orwell's
1984 offers a fictional example of what has been historically true.
In the book, Oceania's success relied on destroying historical
consciousness and societal tradition. Winston Smith was able to
understand and then resist the tyranny of the state because he
maintained a modicum of historical memory, allowing him to see
the pervasive propaganda for what it was. "He remember[ed] a
time when life was different, when social life was not controlled
by the state."[55] This is the anchoring power of tradition—the
collected, cumulative memories of generations past whose
wisdom and experience shape our perspective, giving our life
identity and meaning through the chains of the human family.
Protecting and perpetuating such traditions lead us to recognize,
as Russell Kirk said, "that modern people are dwarves on the
shoulders of giants, able to see farther than [our] ancestors only

because of the great stature of those who have preceded us in time."[56] Our traditions enable our ancestors to pass down ideas and practices that, in F.A. Hayek's words, "embody the experience of many more trials and errors than any individual mind could acquire."[57] Traditions create social strength, something the state loathes. Indeed, its size and scope have increased to the extent that mediating institutions and their traditions have receded from daily life. The weakening of the family and the social acceptance of promiscuity, abortion, and divorce have all been normalized in parallel to the perception that tradition and custom are chains from the past to be shirked off without concern or consequence. The politically independent family resists these trends and recognizes that traditions, properly implemented, are a sort of social strand—each thread itself relatively weak, but when intertwined with others, much stronger. Family dinners, nightly walks, journal writing, date nights, vacations, holiday gatherings, scripture study, expressions of gratitude, acts of service, exercise, reading together, and so many other traditions offer opportunities to develop family strength, discuss ideas, support those who need help, and reinforce social bonds.

- **Act and be free.** Miep Gies was born into a Catholic family in Austria in 1909, but at age eleven was sent to live with a foster family in the Netherlands due to local food shortages and her family's inability to provide for her. At age twenty-four, she became the secretary to Otto Frank, a Jewish man who owned a small company in Amsterdam. It was less than a decade later when, following Germany's invasion of the Netherlands and the heavy restrictions being imposed on its Jewish citizens, Otto and his family went into hiding in an attic apartment behind Otto's business. Miep risked her own life for nearly two years, along with her husband and several of Otto's other employees, to smuggle food, supplies, and news into the secret apartment.

Life was obviously difficult for the Frank family; one of Otto's daughters used writing as her outlet to persevere through the oppression. "The brightest spot of all is that at least I can write down my thoughts and feelings," she wrote, "otherwise I would be absolutely stifled."[58] That girl, Anne Frank, was discovered after twenty-five months in hiding along with her family on August 4, 1944, by the Gestapo. Despite Miep's efforts to liberate them— she went to the police headquarters and tried, unsuccessfully, to bribe the officers to free their prisoners—the occupants were sent to concentration camps. Anne died only six months later, at age fifteen; only Otto survived. Miep did not follow the law—she did what was right. Those are sometimes different choices. It was illegal to hide Anne Frank and her family, to help slaves find freedom in the southern states, and to protest racist government policies. Legality and morality are not synonymous, and politically independent families recognize this truth. They teach their children to do what is right and that sometimes governments and cultures promote, institutionalize, and enforce what is wrong. They recognize that the law is whatever those in power say it is, and sometimes those in power are corrupt and worthy of our disobedience. Politically independent families also recognize that learning history is essential so as to help their children understand the state's past abuses in order to prevent future ones. They do not consider freedom a gift from the state but rather an innate aspect of humanity that must be asserted and, at times, defended from those who wish to undermine it.

The state desires our subjection, not our liberation. It promotes historical illiteracy over an informed citizenry. It thrives on apathy and distraction. It wants to weaken families in order to better capture the minds of the young; it needs to be perceived as a savior instead of a threat, so it must cultivate our dependence. It fashions authority figures (so-called experts) whose opinions are pushed widely onto the public to substitute for their own thinking—an easy task when the public is distracted and scared. To these elite few, the collective public largely outsources its thinking, consequently subordinating their conscience and agency to the few who pull the levers of the political process. Children grow up in this environment, thinking it normal and proper—like growing up in the Matrix without knowing it's a simulation. Everyone around them plays along for the emperor, agreeing he has no clothes—until one child speaks up and says what everyone knew all along. Such independent thoughts and actions are what the state fears most.

INTERDEPENDENCE

As mentioned earlier, those men who signed the Declaration of Independence did so at great risk. But what we previously overlooked in reviewing the story sheds important light on the issue of independence. At the end of the document—after explaining their reasoning for separation from Great Britain and publicly stating their treasonous position—the signers stated that "with a firm reliance on the protection of divine Providence, we mutually pledge to each other our Lives, our Fortunes and our sacred Honor." In the very act of declaring independence, they pledged their interdependence.

As great as political and economic independence is, such freedom must be placed in context—for both colonial delegates throwing off the shackles of royal rule and families rearing children in the shadows of an omnipotent state cannot truly do much of anything entirely on their own. Taken to the extreme, imagine your family stranded on a remote island—akin to the classic novel *The Swiss Family Robinson*. Having to produce what you need for food, clothing, and shelter by yourself would be arduous, if not impossible in some circumstances. And defending yourself from others on the island might be a daunting task if no one comes to your aid; exposure to threats without any allies might lead to your inevitable doom.

It is extremely hard for a family to thrive in isolation, whether in a rare island scenario or routine circumstance common to the modern era, where people aren't alone but are still lonely. Despite being more frequently and easily connected to others than any other generation, 46 percent of Americans report feeling lonely sometimes or always, and 43 percent report feeling isolated from others and without companionship or meaningful relationships.[59] This is excellent news for the state as Hannah Arendt observed in *The Origins of Totalitarianism*: "Terror can rule absolutely only over men who are isolated against each other... Therefore, one of the primary concerns of all tyrannical government is to bring this isolation about."[60] Familial independence is critical, but the context is essential—the independence we're speaking of is from the state, not from one another. Indeed, as a social species, it's critical that children (and adults, of course) form connections with others for mutual support and cooperation. The point is not independence per se but independence from the state and its totalitarian tendencies. This political and economic freedom requires a strong society comprised of interdependent people creating community and connection to ensure that isolated individuals do not become directly dependent upon the state.

Of course, the primary form of interdependence is that within a single family itself, where each member supports one another. This *internal interdependence* fosters a sense of belonging and creates a sort of division of labor, where family members contribute differently; traditionally, the father is the primary breadwinner and protector, while the mother is the nurturer and homemaker. As children mature, they are assigned various tasks and duties to help out around the home and learn the skills needed to be a competent adult and, in turn, a father or mother in their own future family economy. As with any general system, there are exceptions and adaptations required for different circumstances—and even in a totally traditional setting, it would probably be unreasonable to completely divide labor to the point where the father doesn't help clean the home or care for the children, or the mother doesn't have a professional side hustle or other economic activity to contribute to the family income (and insure against the future, should she ever become divorced and thus responsible for her own financial situation). But strong families involve individuals working together, pulling their weight, serving one another, and combining their resources and energies to further the family's goals and the individual success of its members.

We stand on the shoulders of giants, and no family member can claim success in life without attributing that success, in part, to a parent or grandparent. *Generational interdependence* recognizes the influence of grandparents upon grandchildren and the support they can provide to their adult children. This support is reciprocated by those adult children when their elderly parents require extra care as they age. About 70 percent of those aged sixty-five or older lived with their children or children-in-law in the mid-nineteenth century.[61] Multiple generations under one roof were fairly common. And while this living arrangement no doubt comes with its own complexities and controversies, it offers a stronger support structure, more memories, a larger pool of resources to share, and additional role models and mentors for the children. By 1990, however, less than 15 percent of the elderly lived with their children due to a variety of factors: the rapid growth of suburbs designed for nuclear families; the heavy increase in the health and economic well-being of older adults; and prosperous economic circumstances driving the use of retirement centers with professional help for the elderly.[62] Of course, generational interdependence does not require each individual to physically live under the same roof—what's important is the strength of the relationships between relatives, providing the young with the wisdom and insights of their living ancestors and enabling adult children and parents to support one another.

Finally, we are connected through *civic interdependence*—the interfamilial network of unrelated individuals joining together for mutual support and cooperation. Freedom requires responsibility, for a people who do not take care of themselves will soon find themselves being supported by the state at their own expense and to their own ultimate detriment. But families cannot subsist on their own, so a strong society of free individuals helping and trading with one another is the only way to resist the state's authoritarianism. Perhaps the grandest experiment in political and economic freedom— the creation of the United States of America—was essentially a demonstration of this truism. And the strong societal fabric being woven by colonists and waves of new immigrants was so starkly contrasted against the Old World's ways (where those "at the head of some new undertaking" were almost always "the government... or a man of rank"[63]) that Alexis de Tocqueville, in his detailed review of the budding American nation, marveled at the "immense assemblage of associations" he witnessed.

> Americans of all ages, all conditions, and all dispositions, constantly form associations. They have not only commercial and manufacturing companies, in which all take part, but associations of a thousand other kinds—religious, moral, serious, futile, extensive, or restricted, enormous or diminutive.

> The Americans make associations to give entertainments, to found seminaries, to build inns, to construct churches, to diffuse books, to send missionaries to the antipodes; in this manner they found hospitals, prisons, and schools. If it is proposed to inculcate some truth, or to foster some feeling, by the encouragement of a great example, they form a society....

> I have often admired the extreme skill with which the inhabitants of the United States succeed in proposing a common object to the exertions of a great many men, and in inducing them voluntarily to pursue it.[64]

Civic interdependence is how society is created—the free actions of independent people trading with and charitably assisting one another. Unfortunately, many confuse the distinction between society and the state, believing that government programs are synonymous with voluntary associations. They feel absolved from having to put in the effort to create society since they pay taxes so bureaucrats and their hirelings can do the work for them. These people outsource and delegate their responsibilities to the state, thus ignorantly trading away civic interdependence for dependence—as if hens asking the nice-looking fox to help guard their house is a good idea. It is these people who falsely believe they are free, of whom Goethe wrote, saying that "none are more hopelessly enslaved."[65] Not content to work for the real thing, such people shirk society in favor of a forgery. We are all the worse off for it.

Society brings us together, creating a dynamic web of interdependent relationships. Someone in need is thus more likely to have a variety of individuals in their network who can render aid and provide emotional and other support. This unity is the state's kryptonite, for the state's success requires our division and dependence upon it, which comes through weakened social ties—especially those in the family. Arendt's observations about historical totalitarianism, with its need to rule over isolated (and thus not interdependent) people, go beyond matters of politics and economics. Indeed, some might think that isolation is akin to independence itself—a sort of autonomy where someone thinks independently or practices rugged individualism. But that's not what Arendt was getting at. She describes it this way:

> While isolation concerns only the political realm of life, loneliness concerns human life as a whole. Totalitarian government, like all tyrannies, certainly could not exist without destroying the public realm of life, that is, without destroying, by isolating men, their political capacities.[66]

It is this destruction of "the public realm of life" that has most aggressively expanded the state in the modern era—the elimination of the mediating institutions de Tocqueville credited as part of the

American success story. In his era, it was extremely common for those in need to form and join fraternal associations that provided health care, life insurance, and other benefits. More than just "a white male phenomenon,"[67] these organizations were intensely popular among immigrants, minorities, and the working class. Their prime objective was "to promote the brotherhood of man… to establish a system for the care of the widows and orphans, the aged and disabled, and enable every worthy member to protect himself from the ills of life."[68] In 1910, their combined membership surpassed 13 million;[69] observers noted that such organizations "honeycombed the slums of Chicago" and among one ethnic minority, the "number of societies passes computation," while the Lower East Side of Manhattan "swarms with voluntary organizations of many kinds."[70] And this welfare was not simply the product of formal institutions dispensing charity. To the contrary, most of the support came from people in "the public realm of life" informally connecting with and contributing to one another's success:

> Reciprocal relief was far more prevalent than either governmental or private hierarchical relief. Its most basic expression was informal giving, the countless and unrecorded acts of kindness from neighbors, fellow employees, relatives, and friends. The precise magnitude of informal giving can never be known, but it was undeniably vast. A study of 200 wage-earning families in New York City conducted in 1905 revealed that "almost every family of small income received some help or other from friends or relatives in the form of clothing for the children, money for the rent, or occasional gifts to carry the family over a tight place." According to the study, informal giving aided so many that it was fallacious to classify families into distinct categories such as "dependent" or "independent." The assistance provided through church congregations included many elements of reciprocal relief. It often appeared in spontaneous and unrecorded guises. Help came from collection plates and via such monetary intangibles as job information, homes for orphans, barn raising, and temporary housing.[71]

This was interdependence in action, and the state snuffed it out. The rise of the modern welfare state forced fraternal societies into "full retreat as social welfare institutions." By assuming the burden of caring for those in need, "governments had undermined much of the reason for the existence of societies and thus for people to join."[72] The role of churches "shrank dramatically with the expansion in government spending under the New Deal," with the data clearly showing that "higher government spending leads to lower church charitable activity."[73] In fact, church welfare spending "fell by 30 percent in response to the New Deal."[74] As a result, "the old relationships of voluntary reciprocity and autonomy have slowly given way to paternalistic dependency."[75]

Individuals in the modern era have shown increasing indifference to public engagement and civic connection. Organizations such as the Red Cross, Kiwanis, Rotary, and religious institutions of all stripes have seen declines in membership. Many newer organizations boast large numbers of supporters and members, yet unlike their more demanding predecessors, the modern associations involve far less community connection and social bonding. Where people once heavily interacted through their leagues and societies and fraternal organizations, they now mostly affiliate with organizations (if at all) in direct fashion, typically by donating once a year and receiving an email newsletter or attending an event. Social media, for its part, often substitutes human connection with an impersonal, digital veneer of superficial connection—creating opportunity for many more relationships, but each of them weak and lacking much substance. If the tightly knit social fabric is being substituted with loose threads, it will not be able to resist the pressure applied against it. Resisting an omnipotent state aiming to captivate the hearts and minds of our children requires that families seek strength wherever they can find it—internally, from relatives, and from the community. We cannot resist the state's authoritarian actions without supporting one another. Live together, die alone.

NECESSARY NURTURE

"The first thing that a totalitarian regime tries to do is to get at the children, to distance them from the subversive, varied influences of their families, and indoctrinate them in their rulers' view of the world."[1]

—*Supreme Court of the United Kingdom*

W HEN MY WIFE AND I built our home, we designed our backyard to include a large garden area. It was an ambitious undertaking given its size, but we were determined to increase our self-sufficiency and generate a wide range of produce. As the soil became dotted with tiny starter plants, we had visions of abundant, delicious produce overflowing our kitchen counters during harvest time. What we hadn't anticipated were all the challenges our garden would face and the pests and problems we had invited merely by planting things in the ground. In a matter of days, invasive bugs feasted on our tiny plants. Strong windstorms whipped them to death. Irrigation problems starved some of them. Nutrient imbalances in our soil deprived others of what they needed to thrive. What I thought would be "natural" and fairly easy ended up being extremely difficult; it seemed that threats I didn't previously know about or fully appreciate suddenly reared their ugly head to thwart my efforts.

As I experimented with (and largely failed at) backyard gardening, I sometimes thought about the similarities between those efforts and another enterprise I had recently undertaken: parenting. Our two children were very young still, and I was only beginning to learn about the many forces that saw my children as "soft entry points," as one United Nations official called them, by which to propagandize them into supporting the state—to be "born and bred from a young age"[2] into thinking approved thoughts established by the ruling regime. As I would come home from work and survey my garden, I was frustrated at what was happening to my plants in my absence. I couldn't be there all day to monitor each plant, squash each bug, and make micro adjustments as needed; they were exposed while I wasn't near them. How would it be any different with my children? In the years ahead, I knew that my wife and I would not—indeed, *should* not—hover over them incessantly, hoping to fend off the individuals, institutions, and ideas that might wish to harm them for whatever nefarious purposes motivated such people to see children like mine as impressionable recruits for their agenda. I wanted to nurture my plants so they could thrive and produce. I was already failing there, so how could I make sure to nurture my children in an environment full of potential threats?

School wasn't the answer; that much was evident to me. I went to government schools and didn't like the experience very much at all. I detested being forced to learn things I didn't care about in which I found no relevance or purpose. I didn't like how there was typically one approved way of thinking we were required to follow to be graded well. And only later in life did I come to realize how much was simply left out of my education. (Can we really expect the state's schools, as one example, to teach about its many atrocities?) I was not alone in my feeling that so-called public education was substandard and full of problems. Before I ever started as a student, a group of education experts and stakeholders convened a number of meetings and gathered data to review and assess the schooling landscape. In 1983, after eighteen months of study, the National Commission on Excellence in Education released its findings: "The educational foundations of our society are presently being eroded by a rising tide of mediocrity that threatens our very future…"[3] Not exactly a ringing endorsement. They continued:

> If an unfriendly foreign power had attempted to impose on America the mediocre educational performance that exists today, we might well have viewed it as an act of war. As it stands, we have allowed this to happen to ourselves.[4]

The decreasing quality of modern education is a feature, not a bug—just as the actual bugs in my garden were a feature of that environment. The architects of modern schooling—those who created its "nature" to which countless young children are subjected—desired not independence and intellectual curiosity but subordination of the masses to increase power and control. The deliberate dumbing down of the rising generation was intentional in their pedagogical pursuits. The "individual must subordinate himself as a particular person," wrote William Torrey Harris, the longstanding U.S. Commissioner of Education, "and make himself a servant of universal ideas such as he finds already formulated in society and the state."[5] In service of the state, "the individual must lose himself in order that he may find himself."[6] Or, in the words of Johann Gottlieb Fichte—the philosophical father of the Prussian model of education, which became the blueprint for state schools in America and beyond—education's purpose was "to be a reliable and deliberate art for fashioning"[7] children into model citizens for the state, "to which we shall first of all have to turn our expectant gaze."[8] Subordination was the goal, as was Horace Mann's effort to homogenize diverse people into one predictable mass and John Dewey's admiration of the nascent state system of education "to undermine the importance and uniqueness of family life."[9]

I fear that too few of us are thinking about the critical need to truly nurture our children to become independent. Several years ago, I was attending a conference hosted by an organization whose members comprised most of the various "freedom-fighting" non-profits around the world. In one of the presentations, the organization showed a graph that displayed the cumulative budgets of all of these organizations. It was an impressive figure to most of the attendees, I'm sure—tens of millions of dollars being spent annually by these institutions in an effort to promote freedom and shrink the size and scope of the state. But I wasn't impressed; I was disheartened. As I looked at that dollar amount, I questioned what portion of those resources were being allocated toward reaching and teaching young people. I felt as if those of us involved in these organizations are often like gardeners in an orchard full of decaying, diseased trees. Desperate to reclaim them, we heap bucketloads of fertilizer on these aged trees, hoping they return to good health and fruitful production. And while those efforts are no doubt important, any good gardener would also make sure to focus on the seeds and saplings to better ensure that they are spared the same fate as the others. After all, as the saying goes, it's easier to build strong children than to repair broken men. But as important as mediating institutions are in this effort, the family is the primary and ultimate institution responsible for nurturing children.

How well are we parents doing? From teachers and textbooks to TikTok, Twitter, and beyond, our children are bombarded with ideas and information that are often false, sometimes harmful, and usually designed to persuade them toward a certain action and agenda. So many parents feel at a loss at how to push back and protect their children. How can we best nurture our children to withstand these forces? As a novice gardener, I employed whatever countermeasures I could reasonably find to protect my tender plants—fertilizer, pesticide, and barriers to shield them from the strong winds where we live. What can we as parents do to nurture our children and fortify them against the unfriendly forces they'll face?

INTENTIONAL INDOCTRINATION

If you're not going to teach your children, then others will do it for you—and those others will likely hold (and aggressively promote) values opposed to your own. Statist authoritarians have long been quite open and explicit about their desire to influence the rising generation's political, economic, and religious beliefs (and subsequent actions). Communist countries, for example, ran state schools where "from kindergarten onward children [were] indoctrinated with an aggressive form of atheism" and persuaded "to denounce parents who follow religious practices at home."[10] But the state's indoctrination is not reserved only for regimes that are so transparently totalitarian; propaganda permeates the public schools in the United States of America as well, where textbooks sanitize the state's atrocities and downplay the damage caused by elected officials (especially those in the Democratic Party, which 87 percent of high school teachers support[11]). When are students taught details about Mao Zedong's concentration camps, or the living conditions of American citizens of Japanese heritage under FDR's internment camps, or the brutality of Ho Chi Minh? Even the group of people who threw off the shackles of the world's most powerful state— the British Empire—and who crafted a Constitution that sought to substantially limit the size and scope of the state, unlike anything in modern history, are now often attacked in academia and popular culture by people who amplify their imperfections in an attempt to disregard their classical liberal, limited government views.

And it's not just so-called progressive communities pushing for social justice, social-emotional learning, critical race theory, and the like. In my conservative community in Utah, one elementary school featured a wall plastered with left-leaning ABCs; each paper had a large letter with a word and sentence below it to teach kids about words beginning with each letter. Students learned that "W is for woke," "S is for social justice," "A is for activist," and more. Radical messages persuade our impressionable children, even (and perhaps especially) in places we wouldn't expect. These developments must wake us up to the fact that *education is never a value-neutral proposition*; information carries context and will shape not only a child's abilities but his or her worldview as well. *Who* teaches our children and *how* they perceive the world can be more important than *what* they teach since even neutral or apolitical curricula can be twisted by teachers or subtly infused with perspectives and suggestions influencing a child's opinions. A single textbook publisher catering to Texas schools will emphasize, as required by state law, "the free enterprise system and its benefits," whereas for their California customers, they will describe the "yawning gap between the haves and have-nots and what is to be done about it,"[12] while celebrating unions and decrying the concentration of wealth. The same book, when teaching about the Second Amendment, tells California children that court rulings on the issue have allowed for gun control regulations, whereas the version produced for Texas children omits that section entirely.[13] An educational process controlled by politicians is likely to be manipulated to only share information that conforms or appeals to the cultural and political whims of the majority in the community. Even worse, government schools are unlikely to educate the rising generation about the atrocities, deficiencies, and inherent problems with the government, thus omitting truthful information that does not serve the state's aims. And well-meaning teachers, being fallible humans, are likely to perpetuate these problems either due to ignorance or cultural conformity. Education is a process that can be weaponized both by socialist totalitarians and sympathetic teachers of all political stripes.

Parents need to realize that *all* children are indoctrinated. The question we must ask ourselves is what are our children being taught as truth. While indoctrination has a negative connotation, as does propaganda, these words ultimately describe the delivery of information. Through indoctrination, we teach a set of beliefs or truths—the "doctrine." And propaganda is, at its core, simply the propagation of information, passing from one person to the next. These words are typically used in a pejorative sense because of so many situations in which people try, as George Orwell wrote, to "make lies sound truthful and murder respectable, and to give an appearance of solidity to pure wind."[14] When the state's disciples and devotees twist the truth—better put, when they intentionally mislead and lie—we rightly cast this information manipulation in a negative light. But that only works when we know it's happening; over and over, people swallow falsehoods without realizing it. Given the breadth of the state's intellectual reach—with allies and accomplices in academia, media, religion, pop culture, education, and more—it's clear we live amidst a war of ideas. Our children's minds are ground zero for an intellectual battle many parents don't even realize is occurring. Of course, we cannot win a war we don't know is even being fought, so the first step is to wake up to this reality and understand the enemy's nature and goals.

One summer evening as a seventeen-year-old, I was scanning radio stations for something fun to listen to. I shifted frequencies over and over again, not having much success. (This was long before the days of Spotify and other streaming services…) When I finally found something tolerable, I reflected on what was actually happening: my radio antenna (and my body!) was being bathed in radio frequencies every second of every day, transmitted from a variety of broadcast towers. Before then, this constant assault of information was not apparent to me. Think of how much more data is being beamed through the air with all the cell phone towers that have proliferated in our communities! A decade later, as a new parent, this memory returned to me, but in a different context. My toddler son was watching a YouTube video with some dancing puppets—a harmless, fun few minutes we enjoyed together. I then realized that as he and his sister grew up, they would also be bombarded with information and ideas relentlessly—from the media, peers, politicians, and supposed authority figures. I wouldn't be able to stop it; like the pests attacking my garden's plants, there were societal forces I simply could not thwart. It was simply a fact to be recognized and mitigated as best as one could.

We parents can't prevent our children from being exposed to falsehoods and harmful ideas. What we can do is fortify them against that inevitability. Independent families must be intentional about transmitting their ideas and values to their children—teaching them the "doctrine" before the state and its many messengers reach them. This intergenerational transmission of ideas is extremely common when it comes to religious belief; parents often take their children to church, read scripture, pray, and demonstrate how believers think and act so their children can follow suit. But too many parents fail to bring this level of intentionality to political and economic ideas. They surrender their children during their most formative years to the state's schools—then wonder years later why they have become hostile to their parent's ideas and values. After years of helping parents teach their children the ideas of freedom with our *Tuttle Twins* books, I've come to realize the sad truth about why so few parents have been doing this job themselves: they were never taught! Countless parents have told me how much our books taught *them*, the adults who should already know these things. While many parents feel fine sharing their religious beliefs with their children, very few feel competent enough about political and economic ideas to explain them to their children.

Consequently, they don't—so they leave it up to *others* to do it for them. They fail to provide their children a foundation of freedom because their own foundation is so weak. They cannot transmit ideas they themselves do not adequately understand.

After speaking to a group of parents recently, one mother stood up during the Q&A afterward and asked why I felt teaching children about political and economic ideas was so important. "Shouldn't we just let kids be kids?" she asked. In reply, I asked if she felt it was okay for her children to learn about the "birds and the bees" from the internet. Awkward laughter broke out as everyone recognized how ridiculous that would be. Clearly, when it comes to something as important as sexual intimacy, we as parents should convey this information in an appropriate setting, with proper context and an opportunity for our children to safely ask questions. More importantly, we introduce age-appropriate ideas and offer more detail and relevant information as they mature. I pointed out that failing to convey this information properly and at an early age might mean that a child will learn harmful ideas elsewhere, leading to future problems. "We all understand the importance of this process when it comes to explaining how the reproductive system works," I noted. "Why shouldn't we do something similar to explain how the world works?" If we don't nurture our children by introducing age-appropriate ideas about the importance of independence and how the state fights it, they are unlikely to learn from other sources we trust. Children are going to embrace a perspective that colors their understanding of the world; it's not a matter of if but who will share it with them, why, and how. If we want a say in the matter—if we want to help our children learn the truth and be able to evaluate other ideas and philosophies through a lens of liberty—then we have to be proactive about teaching these things to our children. We have to be as intentional in their political and economic indoctrination as many of us are with religious matters.

Think of it this way: every industry needs a pipeline of new customers to thrive. Consumer brands often change up their advertising efforts to ingratiate themselves with younger audiences; their financial health depends on the rising generation finding their products and services appealing. People all around the world have meetings and strategy sessions to determine how they can capture the attention and loyalty of your children—consumer brands like soda drinks, candy, and cookies; companies that produce entertainment, educational services, sports, and even pornography; and especially authoritarians and socialists who entice young people with their alluring promises of free schooling, health care, housing, and more. (The state's efforts here are particularly expansive through its schooling institutions, research grants, welfare programs, and much more.) These individuals use the latest developments in neuroscience and the proliferation of technology to better reach and persuade your children. They often don't share your values or care about your priorities; they have a self-serving purpose of leading your child down their path.

Neglect means surrender. If we aren't intentional about counteracting these coordinated efforts, then we've lost. So, knowing that these individuals exist and are actively trying to influence your children—knowing that the state and its allies want to nurture your child's mind in an opposing direction—what can you do about it? Below are some fundamental yet critical steps each of us can take to build the necessary defenses against these attacks:

- **Eat dinner together.** In the past two decades, the number of families having dinner together has declined by one-third,[15] yet 62 percent of parents with children at home wish they had family dinners more often.[16] Though 84 percent of parents agree that these shared meals are important, only around 50 percent of family dinners are eaten together.[17] Of course, the nutritional value of a healthy dinner is important for a child's development, but family dinners are about far more than feasting at the same time. These experiences create a connection between family members, strengthening the bonds of support that can be critical during future challenges someone in the family may experience. They allow children an opportunity to share what they learned and experienced during the day and receive feedback and critical questions from parents that can help them process what they are feeling. Family dinners also create an intentional situation in which parents can bring up items for discussion or debate, offering a safe environment to challenge ideas, analyze a current event, or convey information to the children that otherwise might be difficult or impossible when everyone is going their separate ways at other times of the day. Eating dinner together helps families create a strong foundation upon which they can build in later years—a fortified structure that will better withstand the inevitable resistance they will face as their children mature and are exposed to and enticed by hostile ideas and individuals.

- **Set goals together.** As individuals, we either act or are acted upon; we can be proactive in creating a life we desire or reactive to the life others impose upon us. Especially when the omnipotent state is so influential in varied aspects of our lives—education, health care, employment, housing, family planning, entrepreneurship, and more—it is important to be intentional in determining how we will navigate the system we're forced to live under to create the best life possible. Parents should model this for their children by identifying and sharing the goals they are pursuing for the family and their own lives. They can encourage their children to do the same and support them in these efforts. This should be thoughtfully done since goal setting can actually inhibit progress if we don't plan the follow-through that will help our goals become a reality; routine failure to achieve goals might discourage children from being goal-oriented and intentional later in life. James Clear, author of the excellent book *Atomic Habits*, notes that "You do not rise to the level of your goals. You fall to the level of your systems."[18] As families, we should create the right home environment, daily routines, micro goals, incentives, and expectations to best ensure we succeed and help our children become independent individuals. Have quarterly reviews with each child to review progress, identify challenges, and plan for the months ahead. Clear's book is a great guidebook to get started.

- **Build relationships with each child.** Those of us with more than one child know, by intimate experience, that each of our children is unique and requires us to parent them differently. We recognize that the way we discipline one of them will be ineffective if applied to another. So we adapt and customize our approach slightly for different children. Similarly, we should customize our experiences with and support for each child. Family vacations, mealtimes, game nights, and other shared experiences are extremely important for creating strong families, but we should not overlook the need to directly connect with each child individually. Parents should plan one-on-one time with each child, either together as a couple or taking turns, to plan activities of specific interest to that child and spend quality time with them. After all, even though each son or daughter is an interdependent part of a family group, they are also an individual with unique desires, challenges, and purpose. By honoring and investing in our child's individual needs, we will help elevate in their mind the importance of their unique identity. The state promotes collectivism and wants to subordinate each child's interests and rights to the whole. It's imperative that we counteract this by helping our kids understand the importance of their individualism.

- **Talk about current events.** Children are going to model the behavior, attitudes, and opinions of *someone* as they slowly develop their own; even as adults, our views are heavily influenced by, if not wholesale adopted from, what others tell us. Independent thinking and analysis are rare; we typically take shortcuts and look to others for social cues and snippets of information to accelerate our opining-forming and understanding of events. Recognizing this reality, we should be proactive about discussing what's happening in the world with our children, even from a young age—because they will be exposed to contrasting ideas and interpretations from others at school, social media, church, friends, family, and more. But more than just sharing our perspective on current events, we should challenge our children to look deeper at what's happening. We need to encourage critical thinking, skeptical questions, and a healthy mistrust of mainstream media narratives serving the state. We need to help our children learn historical examples demonstrating how often people are misled and manipulated in order to manufacture public support for a war, program, or policy that benefits others at our expense. Those who don't learn from the past are condemned to repeat it, so we need to take the initiative to help our children understand history and apply its lessons and warnings to what's happening today.[19]

ACTIONS SPEAK LOUDER

Debra Harrell was in a bind. It was the summer of 2014, and she needed to work her shift at McDonald's. Normally during summer breaks, her nine-year-old daughter Regina would accompany her to work and spend the hours playing on her laptop. But then their home was broken into, and burglars stole the computer. Instead of being bored at a plastic table all day, Regina asked if she could play at the popular nearby park. As a forty-six-year-old single mother, Debra knew her daughter was a responsible girl and that the park was always filled with kids, parents, and caretakers enjoying the splash pad. The town even ran a lunch program there. Every which way, including financially, Debra thought her daughter's old-fashioned request— "It's summer! Can I play outside?"—made sense. So she dropped her daughter off with a cell phone and pocket money, and off to work she went. But on Regina's third day at the park, a woman asked her where her mother was—and upon learning she was at work, dialed 911 to report an abandoned child. Debra was arrested, thrown in jail overnight, and lost custody of her daughter for seventeen days. Despite public outrage and media attention shining a spotlight on what happened, it took two years before the neglect charges were dropped. Debra had faced up to a decade in prison.[20]

Sadly, this story is not unique. All across the country, parents are reprimanded, arrested, or have their children interviewed and sometimes even taken into custody for letting them experience a bit of independence. Natasha Felix was cited for neglect after her three children, aged five, nine, and eleven, played at the park near her home. She checked on them from the window every few minutes, but a passerby noticed the children without an adult and called the Department of Children and Families Services. It took two years of court battles to finally overturn Natasha's neglect charge.[21] Kari Anne Roy was visited by police after a woman marched her six-year-old son home—a mere 150 feet away from where he had been playing alone. Child Protective Services came soon after to interview each of Kari Anne's three children separately, without their parents, asking about unrelated things such as whether they had done drugs or if their parents showed them movies with naked people.[22] Melissa Henderson was charged with criminal reckless conduct for letting her fourteen-year-old care for her four younger siblings. A neighbor called the police after observing the four-year-old, Thaddeus, wandering outside. Days later, Melissa was booked into jail; the deputy sheriff, in his report, wrote that something terrible might have happened to Thaddeus, such as being kidnapped or even "bitten by a venomous snake." Melissa protested that her child had only been gone a few minutes, but the officer responded that a few minutes was all the time a venomous snake needed.[23]

Chances are, you experienced more childhood freedom than your own offspring do. As a child of the '80s, I recall wandering far distances from my home without parental supervision; Mom had no clue where I was. There were no tracking devices, smartwatches, or cell phones to monitor my whereabouts. Many of us in that era knew simply to be home when the sun started to set. Reflecting on this stark contrast between our own upbringing full of freedom and the limited amount our children experience today, one columnist said, "I loved it, but it's impossible to imagine letting my own children do this. What happened?"[24] The answers to that question are numerous: social media making it easier to spread scary stories, despite crime and child abduction being lower today than in decades past; a proliferation of technological crutches to support and surveil children, enticing parents to monitor them as obsessively as they do with their social media notifications; a weaker community culture where neighbors don't know or trust one another, thus elevating perceived stranger danger; and numerous other influences that all encourage parents to hover over their children like a helicopter. Yet many parents admit that their natural instinct is to provide their children with more independence; however, they second-guess those inclinations for fear of being mistaken by others as neglectful.[25]

In all of this, we can't ignore the prevailing emotion in play: fear. It is safer for children to roam the streets today than when we were growing up,[26] but many parents are paralyzed either by perceived dangers or the threat of punishment by the state simply for providing their children a modicum of freedom. This cultural conditioning encourages children to follow the rules, do what they're told, stay where they know it's safe, and defer to authorities as to what actions are proper. A generation raised this way becomes a submissive citizenry, ever fearful of supposed dangers and willing to listen to the "experts." We saw it during the response to COVID-19, with people quickly surrendering their freedoms in hopes of being kept safe, putting ineffective cloths on their face, and injecting themselves with experimental substances simply because those in charge said these things were important to be protected. Fear of a perceived danger led millions of people to act irrationally in ways they otherwise never would have, deferring to and not questioning the counsel and orders of the state's emissaries. It was all an exercise in dependence and a remarkable growth in government that increased both the size and scope of the state.

The state wants us to be afraid because we will look to it for safety and security. We are more malleable and easily manipulated when we are scared. We become acted upon rather than acting on our own. By contrast, the greatest threat to the state is a confident, independent-minded individual that acts—often unpredictably, coloring outside the lines set out by the state's central planners. Such people are rule breakers instead of followers, refusing to salute obediently when others submit. They recognize, as Thomas Jefferson said, that it is tempting for many people to "prefer the calm of despotism to the tempestuous sea of liberty."[27] We are persuaded to seek safety by exchanging our liberty in return. The response from authorities to COVID-19 was a ridiculous effort to eliminate risk—to shut down society unless and until the virus was eradicated. "If it can save just one life…" became the mantra guiding those in charge, echoing justifications cited by every totalitarian to suppress individual choice and personal freedom in an effort to reshape society in their vision.

Like us adults, children *need* risk to learn from and evaluate their actions. Danger can't be eliminated, except in some kind of dystopian authoritarian regime wherein people aren't allowed to do anything that would negatively impact others in any way. (Of course, that type of impossible system would create its own obvious dangers.) By measuring risk, we can develop coping skills, challenge our abilities, increase our strength, and allocate resources prudently. In essence, life is one constant series of risk calculations as we determine what we will do. And along the way, the state tries to centrally plan society and create all sorts of plans and programs to reduce or eliminate that risk, such as school systems, welfare programs, and more. But risk mitigation is attached with heavy strings, for the state doesn't try to shield people from the rough and tumble of life out of the goodness of its nonexistent heart. Those who benefit from the state's largesse and support its systems find themselves losing what ultimately matters most: their individual autonomy and self-determination.

Even in school at a young age, children are bombarded with expectations imposed upon them by the state—all in an effort to mitigate the perceived risk of not obtaining sufficient education to succeed later in life. They are expected to learn certain things in a certain way at a certain time, for reasons unknown, because someone else decided that every eight-year-old should know that the mitochondria are the powerhouse of the cell, and every thirteen-year-old should memorize the quadratic equation. Your child might ask the teacher (or you, if they are homeschooled) why they need to learn such things, only to be told that they will be useful at some future time (which, of course, is rarely true). Each child's curiosities are disregarded in favor of what the collective is expected to know and do. Children in this situation are like passengers on a bus representing their life with someone else driving in a direction the child doesn't know or have a say in. Think, by contrast, of how children feel when they first get behind the wheel of a vehicle (for the young ones, sitting on a parent's lap). They are thrilled at the newfound opportunities before them and the control they've been entrusted with. These are the feelings they should experience when it comes to their own life. Their educational and developmental path should be laid out in consultation with them, not imposed upon them based on someone else's expectations. They should have an opportunity to take things in a direction they desire—to explore, fail, be curious, and meander a bit. And later in life, when they encounter central planners and politicians who want to make them follow the state determined path, your children will be able to forge their own because it's what they've been doing for decades. Independence will be something they experience gradually, starting at a young age—not something that magically manifested when they became a legal adult.[28]

- **Lengthen the leash.** Children need to learn independence by practice, which implies failure. They need the opportunity to make mistakes, scrape their knees, and get lost. The alternative, of course, is a generation full of incompetent individuals who have grown used to being coddled and guided by a paternal system—a recipe for societal disaster, no doubt. So let your kids go play at the park alone or cross a busy intersection without your supervision. Teach them what's needed, but then let them spread their wings a bit. Allow them the opportunity to develop the confidence they need to push further. Independence is an intoxicating thing; experiencing a little bit leads to a desire for more.

- **Give your children some control.** A plant that's watered and fertilized too much won't invest the energy into developing a strong root system in search of those nutrients. Similarly, if you plan your child's life and make all their decisions, they won't build the intellectual and emotional muscles needed to determine on their own what direction their life should take. So put your child in the driver's seat of their own life, with whatever boundaries are necessary for their age and maturity level. Ask them what *they* want to learn. Give them the freedom to fill their time pursuing projects they're curious about. Let them pick what they'll wear and how they'll spend their money. Empower them to make early choices in how their life will develop, and they'll develop a far stronger desire—and more experience preparing—for independence in their adult life.

- **Inspire, don't require.** If we are trying to raise children to become free and independent adults, we have to employ methods that will be conducive to that end. Forcing a child to learn or do something inhibits their individuality and dampens their passion. It destroys their love of learning to be coerced and made to memorize things without personal meaning or seeming relevance to them. On the spectrum between persuasion and coercion, too many parents opt for the latter, falling into parenting styles and personality traits that they were raised with—a command and control approach that asserts dominance to get things done efficiently and as envisioned by the person in charge. While this approach might yield superficial results in the short term by obtaining compliance, it is not an effective way to achieve our long-term goal of raising independent children. We should inspire our children to do what we think is right, giving them space to investigate and make their own choices (and mistakes). They need the autonomy to own their outcomes—and sometimes, those might be different and better than what we as parents first envisioned.

- **Be the change you wish to see.** Can a child learn to become independent if her parents are not? We must model for our children what it looks like since they are far more likely to mimic our actions than modify their behavior because of our words alone. Instead of trusting authority or doing as we are told, we should do our own research and make an informed decision about what we should do. We shouldn't follow the latest fads or do what our peers suggest is proper—we should reject collectivist thinking and try to be intentional in everything we do, informed by our own knowledge and desires. We need to think and act rationally, always skeptical of those in power trying to manipulate our emotions to induce us to believe and act in ways they prefer; we need to act by faith instead of fear. Our children need to see us embrace the tempestuous sea of liberty with confidence.

If we value our children's independence, we have to recognize that our actions speak louder than our words. We can't proclaim the virtues of freedom only to deny it to our children during their most formative years. We can't pretend to be skeptical of authority or frustrated with authoritarians abusing their power and restricting our rights if we emulate in the four walls of our home the problems we perceive outside of it. If we want to raise independent thinkers and doers, then they have to see us as parents exhibit those traits, and we have to provide our children with opportunities to slowly develop them for themselves. Parents concerned about collectivism and the power of the state to negatively impact their children need to offer them incremental independence at a young age so they can become their own thinkers instead of obedient rule followers. Exiting the conveyor belt everyone is mindlessly on requires more than mere words. Sometimes you have to jump.

CULTIVATE SELF-OWNERSHIP

Ayn Rand's famous 1957 novel *Atlas Shrugged* portrays a dystopian future in which the United States of America has degraded into a socialist system that chases away the hard-working capitalists whose innovations and abilities helped make the country's economic engine progress. The story is one big battle between characters who create value and wealth through their effort and determination (the producers) and others whose income and lifestyle depend on using force (the looters and moochers). In the decades since the book was written—and especially in recent years—many people have been shocked to see its fictional plot lines increasingly becoming a reality. As in the book, today's producers, whether big or small, are demonized and attacked for their success; an entire "anti-work" movement has exploded, driven by a seductive (though ignorant) ideology that "questions the need to work for a living."[29]

Producers offer their goods through voluntary trade and seek to solve others' problems by creating products and services that improve our lives. Those hurling the grenades at the producers are the looters and the moochers. Looters are primarily those who become part of the state and use its power to seize wealth from and control producers by passing laws and regulations that impose upon them the state's vision for the way things ought to be. Looters personally profit from their plunderous activities, and their own power and prestige expand as they expand the state's control over producers. They are supported in this effort by the moochers, who vote them into power in exchange for promised perks such as stimulus checks, subsidies, grants, bailouts, jobs, and more. Moochers are the masses who are seduced into living at the expense of others, tasking the looters with maintaining and expanding opportunities that facilitate this leech-like drain on the productive class.

Anyone paying attention to today's state of affairs recognizes that our society is full of moochers, the government is full of looters, and the producers among us are playing defense. We live in an age where "more Americans work for the government than in manufacturing, farming, fishing, forestry, mining, and utilities combined."[30] Trillions of dollars are taken from taxpayers, redistributed to those who didn't earn them, and siphoned along the way by looters whose careers are sustained by the expropriation. And while earlier generations were strenuously opposed to being dependent upon the state and becoming "paupers" by accepting welfare from others, today, there is little cultural resistance to government entitlements and a system of socialist redistribution and individual dependency. (If anything, such dependency is now normalized and even glorified.) How did this happen? How did the state turn a society of fiercely independent, self-reliant individuals into a class of looters and moochers? And how can we as parents nurture our children to become producers and help ensure their prosperity and independence are not undermined by the state and its legion of parasitic supporters?

The cultural transformation in favor of dependence has been methodical and incremental and implemented through a series of seductive enticements. First, the state masks its actions of compulsion in charitable clothing. It claims its programs help the needy and justifies its coercive taxation on the basis that it helps the less fortunate. Producers who resist are branded as selfish contributors to "wealth inequality" for failing to "be patriotic"[31] by paying their "fair share." (Of course, it is the state's agents who get to determine what constitutes fairness.) By claiming that its coercive wealth confiscation is a moral act, the state creates a class of moochers who see their entitlement mentality not as evidence of any greed and sloth but of virtue. Beyond welfare, additional entitlements also expand the moocher class: subsidized housing and artificially low interest rates to help people live in homes they couldn't otherwise afford; grants and guaranteed loans to pay for tuition that otherwise would be too costly; industries and businesses bailed out and propped up through subsidies and stimuli; and many other handouts that encourage freeloaders and financial dependence by people whose actions are distorted by these economic incentives.

Benjamin Franklin once wrote that "those who would give up essential liberty to purchase a little temporary safety deserve neither liberty nor safety."[32] So it is with the state offering supposed financial security in exchange for a reduction of freedom. People are promised to be taken care of should they become poor, sick, or old; the social safety net will catch these people, we are told, by a beneficent government. And the price is our independence. But the looters aren't content with a traditional welfare state—their dominion has grown to include state-operated industries, such as government schools with entrenched teachers' unions, and economic systems that enrich them, such as taxpayer-funded pension funds showering them with revenue far in excess of market rates. When the few live at the expense of the many—or the many at the expense of the few—what becomes of their character? How can a society function when everyone tries to live at the expense of everyone else, with no respect for the rights of others?

What Rand was writing about was the critical importance of self-ownership—and, consequently, the emptiness of soul that comes from its abandonment. To be independent, we must be responsible for ourselves and our actions; we cannot be free if we expect others to care for us and absolve us of the consequences of our actions. Self-ownership, like independence more broadly, is both a mindset and a set of behaviors we as parents can model for our children:

- **Do not force affection.** It's common for parents to push their children to give Grandma a kiss or hug a relative. When that child digs in their heels, some parents press the issue and override the child's reluctance, effectively forcing them to be affectionate. Naturally, we want our children to show the people in their lives that they love them. We recognize that affection is an important part of human interaction, especially between family members. We want what's best for the members of our family; we want our children to have healthy relationships. But forcing our children to be affectionate can be counterproductive and breed resentment. While the goal is noble, the means employed require compelling our children to suppress their natural inclinations and preferences regarding their body. Self-ownership, at its most basic level, implies ownership over your body and being able to control what you do with it through consent. What message are we sending as parents if we are telling our children to ignore their autonomy and submit their body to the dictates of another?

- **Let them suffer the consequences.** Many parents hover over their children, trying to shield them from themselves. I recall an experience from high school when a friend crashed his truck. He was being reckless, and the accident was his fault. Within three days, he was driving a brand-new truck; his parents had replaced the vehicle without imposing any kind of punishment at all. They deprived their son of a learning opportunity and failed to help him experience the consequences of his actions. Where possible, consequences should be tied to the misbehavior; if a child makes a mess with his toys, for example, he should be required to clean them up. But it's also critical that we as parents focus on positive consequences as well as the negative ones. Life isn't just about avoiding pain—we need to identify how to pursue peace and pleasure through productive and beneficial behavior. Focusing on cause and effect in this way will help our children better take ownership of their actions and think about the consequences of their actions, both on themselves and those around them.

- **Defer to their decisions about themselves.** Within reason, parents should accommodate and work around the desires of their children that pertain to their personal behavior. For example, if your daughter doesn't want a nap, perhaps it's best not to force the issue. If your son isn't hungry when you have scheduled dinner time, maybe it's okay to let him eat later. Empowering our children with control should obviously come with boundaries, but we parents can be far more flexible than we typically want to be. We may be inclined to keep an orderly schedule and dictate how things will operate in the home, but raising children in an authoritarian manner does not help us promote and pursue family independence. If we force our children to do things they don't want to, we are employing various levels of aggression against them—and teaching them that this is a proper means to achieve desired ends. In effect, we are validating, in the eyes of our children, the state's approach toward manipulating people.

In the ancient world, a person's life path was largely predetermined by their birth and social standing. It was only in recent centuries that an intellectual revolution led people to see the importance of people being able to choose their own life path—that we own ourselves as well as our minds and hearts. John Locke, in his *Second Treatise on Government*, points out that "every man has a property in his own person: this no body has any right to but himself."[33] To create dependence, then, the state—assisted by the moocher and looter classes that uphold it—must squash self-ownership. Asserting omnipotent power requires a people who do not value or experience this fundamental right. Consider what happens in *The Americans*, a TV show about Soviet spies during the Cold War. Elizabeth Jennings, one of the spies, is given an order from the KGB to begin training her fifteen-year-old daughter, Paige, to similarly become a spy. This is deeply troubling for Elizabeth, whose daughter thinks she's simply a travel agent. She objects, explaining that she chose the life of a spy due to her commitment to communist ideals, but her daughter should similarly have a choice (self-ownership). Elizabeth's Moscow-based handler disagrees, saying, "We don't belong to ourselves; we belong to the world."[34] (Unsurprisingly, it is the KGB who appoints unto themselves the power and responsibility to determine what the collective wants and expects.) Real-world Soviet propaganda was clear on this matter. As one official said, "The education of children in the spirit of communism is a civic obligation of Soviet parents."[35] Or, in the words of another, "Parents must instill in their children… readiness to lay down their life at any moment for their socialist country."[36] For her part, Elizabeth's choice to submit to the state came with a consequence—the renunciation of her parental claims on Paige; the communists demand loyalty to the point of giving up your own child since nothing belongs to the individual. The "world," or the collectivists who appoint themselves its arbiters, owns it all.

Locke points out what we all know about our parental purview over our children: as our children grow up, they gain more independence and self-ownership. "The bonds of this subjection," he writes, "are like the swaddling clothes they are wrapt up in, and supported by, in the weakness of their infancy: age and reason as they grow up, loosen them, till at length they drop quite off, and leave a man at his own free disposal."[37] But too many parents assert their ownership and control until their children become adults, forced into a world without any meaningful experience of making decisions, experiencing consequences, and understanding what self-ownership looks like. Our task is to model and implement this in our children's younger years, making it a natural transition into becoming a free and independent adult. Only with this level of intentionality will we counter the moocher and looter classes and help our children steer clear of their seductive invitations to join them. By instilling self-ownership into our children, we will be in a better position to shrink the state, raising a generation of producers who embrace accountability for their actions. This is how we create independent families to counter the omnipotent state. This is the backbone of the resistance.

THE RESISTANCE

"We must always take sides. Neutrality helps the oppressor, never the victim. Silence encourages the tormentor, never the tormented."[1]

– Elie Wiesel

YOUR BODY IS UNDER a constant barrage of attacks from pathogens such as viruses, bacteria, and fungi. All around you, these microscopic organisms are attempting to invade and incubate themselves. Fortunately, there are various lines of resistance to protect your health and ward off infection.

The first line of resistance protecting your health is your skin—the largest organ which serves as a barrier between your body and these pathogens. It features several layers of cells that self-organize to maintain a waterproof and tightly knit network with beneficial bacteria that help fight invading organisms. But your body also has several points of entry that allow pathogens to penetrate. To ward off infection here, tears, mucus, and saliva break down the cell wall of many bacteria—or trap them inside where stomach acid can then destroy them. Special cells line and protect the nose, throat, and other passages within your body. And for any pathogens evading these multilayered defenses, your body's internal immune system marshals lymphocytes, monocytes, basophils, eosinophils, and neutrophils— collectively known as white blood cells—to respond and return the body to homeostasis. In short, you are regularly protected through multiple layers of resistance to help repel constant attacks that you are typically unaware even exist.

Multilayered resistance is just as critical for known threats and has been the basis for a wide range of successful opposition efforts. Consider as one example the strategic effort launched by Mahatma Gandhi to overturn the longstanding British rule over India. In determining how best to fight off their oppressors, Gandhi and his allies committed early on to a form of nonviolent disobedience they called *satyagraha* or insistence upon truth. Gandhi decided to center the campaign around a protest against the British Salt Act which, for several decades, created a British monopoly on the production and sale of salt, limiting its distribution to government officials and imposing a tax on Indians buying it. On March 12, 1930, Gandhi and a few dozen associates began a daily march toward the Indian coast, where salt was freely available through the evaporation of salt water. Over the next 24 days, the group traversed 239 miles and was joined along the way by thousands of others. Gandhi gathered salt and publicly broke the law, sparking a wave of similar civil disobedience by millions of people across India in the following weeks. Tens of thousands of people were arrested, including Gandhi.[2] This resistance had multiple layers to it: the public sympathy and support among Indians; the widespread publicity of the civil disobedience to draw attention; the condemnation from the international community; the support of the local political system; the involvement of women for the first time in a political struggle; and a strategic plan for successive demonstrations to pressure the British.

Novak wrote that the resistance against totalitarianism features the family as the first line, and this is true; the primary defense against the omnipotent state to protect our children is an economically and politically independent family comprised of parents who are intentional and earnest in their efforts to shield and support their children. But this barrier, like human skin, can often break; abusive or apathetic parents, divorce, fatherlessness, and many more substandard situations create conditions in which children are not given the protection they need. The social fabric is weakened as a result of these conditions, much like the chance of infection increases if one's body has several lacerations. Consequently, our resistance to the state needs a backup plan and supporting strategies to raise children right.

The next line of resistance to protect our children is obviously the extended family—the generational interdependence mentioned earlier. The 55 percent decline over a century of grandparents living with a child and their family is worthy of note,[3] to be sure, though extended family can step in to help even if they live down the road or in another city. Especially for single parents, supporting relatives can fill a void by providing fatherly advice, maternal encouragement, financial aid, educational training, and more. Even for children being raised by both parents, the support structure of caring relatives provides exposure and perspective beyond that of the parents—and sometimes, these influences can have more of a positive impact on a particular child. Reinforcing the relationships between extended family members creates a shared responsibility, family culture, and stronger bonds to help children navigate the world they're growing up in.

Beyond family, close friends and community members can step in to help a child's development and support parents in creating a better family situation. The primary growth mechanism for the state is the so-called social safety net—the (false) perception that it is needed to help people survive. The state thrives when called upon to educate children, provide health care, offer housing, subsidize businesses, feed people, and more. Historically and traditionally, this has been the role of mediating institutions—the civic interdependence mentioned earlier featuring neighborly associations banding together to help one another.

While fraternal societies and charitable organizations were the typical means of providing this support, it can also come in different forms. For example, trade is an effective means of creating a strong society—and where it is restricted or overregulated, black markets are a wonderful way to directly help others get what they need—whether it's something as controversial as a prohibited firearm for self-defense or something as commonplace as banned backyard chickens or providing a lasagna to a neighbor cooked in an uninspected kitchen without first obtaining a food handler's permit. Another line of resistance is the development of an alternative education system outside the propaganda programs pushed by the state—even in locales where homeschooling is heavily regulated or altogether banned. Efforts to help children learn the truth amid a sea of confusion are critical to empowering parents to support their children. To that end, intrepid journalists who speak truth to power and publicly proclaim the proverbial emperor's lack of clothes are an essential line of resistance, for how can families know where the enemy is attacking if no one sounds the alarm?

Families need support to fight the state, and the resistance requires all of us to work together. We must weave a strong social fabric if we want it to be impenetrable to the state's persistent attacks, just as our body's skin has several layers of interlocking cells protecting us. If we want to fight welfare, we need charitable associations that offer help to those in need. If we want to fight the state-sanctioned licensing of abortion, we need to create pregnancy resource centers and support mothers in crisis. If we want to combat propaganda, we need well-funded truth tellers who can create large platforms to call out the media manipulators. If we don't want our money debased, we need to popularize and utilize less corruptible alternatives such as Bitcoin. If we want families to flee government schools, we need to create compelling alternatives. The responsibility is ours to build the resistance, and each of us is needed.

WHAT RESISTANCE LOOKS LIKE

The naked individual should be shielded from the state by multilayered lines of resistance—that much we know. A strong defense is critical given the state's seeming omnipotence. But what are the state's defenses in this fight? How does it protect its power? Recall that when Morpheus explained to Neo how the Matrix operates, he said that the businessmen, teachers, carpenters, and others around him were the "very minds of the people we are trying to save"—and yet because they were not ready to be unplugged and were "so hopelessly dependent on the system,"[4] they would fight to protect it. They would fight the very people trying to save them, falsely thinking that their salvation lay in the system they had grown accustomed to. Our resistance against the state is similar in that our ideological (and at times physical) opposition comes from the local PTA president, the popular mayor, or the strident rabble-rousers in the neighborhood Facebook group. The state is not, of course, an independent entity separate from the people who comprise it; it is the collective power and priorities of those who have chosen to participate in it. It is our friends and neighbors who seem nice and have good intentions but who elect to secure their happiness through an instrument of oppression. It is the systematization and legal justification of mooching, enabling your neighbors to live at your expense.

Knowing who we are resisting, what is it exactly we are fighting against? We have reviewed the nature of the state, the threats to independence, the rampant mooching and incentives to live a life at others' expense, and more. What does this mean on a more practical level? What do the resistance fighters among us need to look out for?

Consider a few examples. First, we should resist the dissolution of the family unit; children need fathers and mothers who are present, caring, supportive, and who are intentional in their educational efforts to empower them as they mature. Abandonment or divorce, whether due to abuse, infidelity, apathy, or otherwise, is like cutting your skin as an open invitation for pathogens to attack; shrinking the state requires strong families, and strong families only exist when both parents pull their weight and commit to one another each day. Another point of resistance is the calendar; an overextended schedule can lead to family distance and weakness. Families should create activities and memories together, which means prioritizing them in the schedule on a regular basis—both organized activities and informal time to allow for spontaneity and flexibility. When family members' busy lives mean they are always going their separate ways, children can be deprived of the nurturing they need to be strong enough to venture out in the world alone. Families who play together resist the state together.

We need to also resist the doom-and-gloom attacks on having children, for strong families are first predicated on procreation. The latest wave of demographic destabilization comes from those experiencing "climate change anxiety" who wonder, like the once-prestigious journal *Lancet*: "Knowing the carbon footprint of a child throughout its life . . . is it acceptable to have a child?"[5] Citing a supposed (but not documented) "scientific consensus" on the matter, Congresswoman Alexandria Ocasio-Cortez told her followers that this apocalyptic view of the world "lead[s] young people to have a legitimate question: Is it okay to still have children?"[6] Despite his jet-setting lifestyle contributing plenty of carbon to the atmosphere, Prince Harry publicly committed to only two children. "I always think to myself, whenever there's another natural disaster, a huge increase in volcano eruptions or earthquakes or flooding, how many clues does nature have to give us before we actually learn, or wake ourselves up to the damage and the destruction that we're causing?"[7] But the idea that one's creation of more children is a contributor to the so-called "climate crisis" is not a view held only by privileged liberals and elite grandstanders. One woman observed this increasing trend among her peers: "Several of my friends feel a child brought into the world now would not have a secure future. They don't want their kids to inherit an unstable world." A third of Americans, when asked why they had or expected to have fewer children than their "ideal number," cited worries about climate change.[8] Fear, spread by the state's "science" ambassadors, is an apparently effective form of coercive birth control. It is seen in book titles like *One Child: Do We Have a Right to More?* and *Toward a Small Family Ethic: How Overpopulation and Climate Change Are Affecting the Morality of Procreation.* And it weakens the size and strength of the family unit itself. A resistance is a numbers game; a fighting force with too few members will not prevail. Perhaps one of the greatest ways to fight the state is for freedom-minded families to reject this fear and procreate prolifically.

As described earlier, we must also resist the tempting offer for aid from the state. Like a drug dealer offering a free sample first, the ultimate aim is dependence; an addicted individual is a reliable customer. To grow, the state must be needed—therefore, it eagerly offers "free" schooling, health care, housing, food, and more to any who claim a need. If you lump all the federal welfare programs together, nearly one in three Americans are dependent upon the state[9]—a statistic approaching 90 percent if you throw in government schooling.[10] Yet 74 percent of voters think Americans "rely too much on the government and not enough on themselves"[11]—an odd inconsistency that shows the clear difference between stated preferences (what people claim to want) and revealed preferences (what people actually want, as evidenced by their actions). As economist Robert Higgs explains, the more dependent people become on the state, the less influence they are likely to have in shrinking or opposing it: "Fear of losing their government benefits effectively neutralizes them in regard to opposing the regime on whose seeming beneficence they rely for significant elements of their real income."[12] Moochers aren't fighters, so the resistance needs to purge its ranks of those who depend upon the state. We must see the outstretched arm of the state for what it is: a sticky tentacle eager to ensnare us upon first contact.

Just as we should protect our body from physical pathogens, we need to resist ideological infection as well—the viral spread of popular but harmful ideas that lead our children to support the state and become culturally ingrained in its traditions to help perpetuate its power. This includes the belief that government is benevolent rather than barbarian—for as Ronald Reagan once quipped, "The nine most terrifying words in the English language are 'I'm from the government and I'm here to help.'"[13] It also includes the idea that the state should "spread democracy" abroad and use military might to impose itself on other people or that taxation is the price we pay for living in a (supposedly) civilized society. We should help our children resist the seductive lure of socialism by understanding what effect it ultimately has beyond the initial distribution of cheap or free goods and services. We can shrink the state by opposing the idea that education is a "common good," justifying the proliferation of government propaganda centers funded at our expense. We need to persuade our children to avoid envy and entitlement, for this is how moochers are made. They need to reject victimhood, an increasingly popular mentality that abandons personal accountability and instead solicits the state's support to redress grievances and impose equity. Our children need to understand that no one owes them anything, that no one should be guaranteed a "living wage," and that the social safety net—while sounding nice in theory—is a dangerous snare that traps too many.

Of course, every atrocity committed by totalitarian regimes and authoritarian individuals resulted from an initial idea—the bitter fruit of a bad seed that took root where it shouldn't have. As Ayn Rand once wrote, "Power-lust is a weed that grows only in the vacant lots of an abandoned mind."[14] Therefore, our resistance must oppose historical illiteracy, for those who don't learn from the mistakes of the past are doomed to repeat them. As the German philosopher Hegel said, history shows that people "never have learned anything from history, or acted on principles deduced from it."[15] Ignorant people are more easily duped, for they are unable to recognize in present situations any patterns from the past that might lead them to reject the state's repeated encroachment on our freedom. So well known is the civic ignorance of the American people—a majority of them would fail a simple U.S. citizenship test[16]—that one well-known writer called the country the *United States of Amnesia*.[17] And while polls and public videos highlight the embarrassing display of adults who lack basic historical knowledge, a true resistance shouldn't just memorize names and dates from the past; we must learn the philosophies, ideas, and values that guided intelligent individuals whose actions we might emulate to improve our own circumstances. We need to think radical thoughts and understand strategy; we need to understand how past societies fell and what the causes were; and we need to recognize how people were previously taken advantage of so we might prevent the same today. History is important precisely because it gives us a context for our own life journey, much as a map is needed to guide one's actions when traveling to a new destination. Thomas Jefferson's observation that people can't be both "ignorant and free"[18] also works in the inverse: people can't be both informed and shackled to the state. Knowledge about the past is how the resistance can fight for a freer future.

Finally, resistance requires the right mindset—a functioning psychological rudder to guide the ship. We have to see ourselves as capable, confident, and courageous as opposed to being a victim or feeling inadequate or dependent. And we need to guard our emotions and be extra cautious when fearful, knowing that we are most easily manipulated when scared of a perceived threat. Despite the apparent omnipotence of the state, we need a mindset that helps us realize our own influence and power; as Thoreau once said, "What a man thinks of himself, that it is which determines, or rather indicates, his fate."[19] And with apologies to Henry Ford, "Whether you think you can [resist the state] or you think you can't, you're right."[20] Mindset matters because psychological warfare precedes actual warfare; the state's prevalent use of propaganda to influence our opinions, emotions, and attitudes makes actual conquest easier. If a subjugated citizenry invites you to "save" them and welcomes your rule, you don't need to conquer them by force. And instead of the state having to fight off the resistance, an easier method is to divide the citizenry and turn their "law-abiding" peers against them.

Katniss Everdeen found herself having to produce propaganda to counter that of the Capitol, the ruling regime in Panem, which ensured that the citizenry had ubiquitous access to televisions by which they could consume the steady stream of state-approved media. The psychological battles in *Hunger Games* were a struggle to win people's minds in order to undermine—and in the Capitol's case, perpetuate—President Snow's perceived power. This fictional representation of mental manipulation viscerally resonates with audiences because it is so central to how the state operates. On the extreme end, for example, the Nazis issued a 1933 decree called the "Ordinance to Deter Insidious Discrediting of the National Government," which required Germans to report those who spoke against the party, its leaders, or the government. The new mandate had the effect of silencing the opposition and weaponizing relationships, leading family members, friends, and neighbors to report one another to the authorities if they dared to demonstrate any level of resistance to the ruling elite. Among countless other examples of citizen informants that might be cited,[21] consider an earlier era closer to home, when President John Adams signed into law the Sedition Act, which authorized punishing those deemed a threat or who published "false, scandalous, or malicious writing" against the U.S. government, one congressman presciently warned:

The country will swarm with informers, spies, delators and all the odious reptile tribe that breed in the sunshine of a despotic power… [T]he hours of the most unsuspected confidence, the intimacies of friendship, or the recesses of domestic retirement afford no security. The companion whom you most trust, the friend in whom you must confide, the domestic who waits in your chamber, all are tempted to betray your imprudent or unguarded follie; to misrepresent your words; to convey them, distorted by calumny, to the secret tribunal where jealousy presides—where fear officiates as accuser and suspicion is the only evidence that is heard.[22]

We are in a war of ideas, and we will lose every battle we do not understand is even being fought. The state's strongest emissaries in this conflict are our neighbors and friends—fellow citizens who become cult-like believers in the state's propaganda and help protect its power by opposing those who resist. While we try to shield our children from the state and guide our families to become economically and politically independent, we need to recognize that the freedoms we typically fight for—speech, assembly, self-defense, autonomy, privacy, and more—are mere outgrowths of our internal attitudes and desires. To oppose the state, we must believe it to be our opponent. To seek a solution, we must recognize the problem. To desire true freedom, we must understand why it is important and envision what life could be like if we had it. Our actions are an extension of our thoughts; our fight against the state is, therefore, inherently intellectual. A resistance not based on sound ideas is one that will not be sustained.

FOUR THINGS TO DO

In the sixth century BC, Sun Tzu was a Chinese military general serving King Helü. An expert strategist as a result of various battles he fought in, Sun compiled his insights into a book, *The Art of War*—

one that advocates diplomacy and building relationships as much as it expounds on how to be victorious in combat. The book became widely read throughout China in the years that followed, especially during tumultuous wars waged among the various Chinese states and spread to Japan, Vietnam, Korea, and other Asian countries. In the twentieth century, *The Art of War* spread to the Western world, and its teachings are often incorporated by American military leaders. But the book's insights go beyond battle and relate to a variety of competitive endeavors, including politics, sports, and business.

"All warfare is based on deception," one of his many strategies suggests—a recognition of the prevalent propaganda used to ensure victory.[23] Another shows the power of restraint in selectively choosing battles: "He will win who knows when to fight and when not to fight."[24] And demonstrating the power of guerrilla warfare against standing armies and bureaucratic battalions, he wrote, "Attack [the enemy] where he is unprepared, appear where you are not expected." The element of surprise is a critical one for those seeking to gain advantage over the opposition. These and countless other observations about military strategy—with their applications far beyond the battlefield—have been put into practice by government, business, and cultural leaders across the world.

How might they help your family? We, too, need a strategy manual to advise us on tactical maneuvers and opportunities to pursue. And if some of these lessons are being used by the opposition, then we better understand them ourselves in order to minimize their effectiveness. The resistance against the state by independent families will better succeed if informed by some strategic guidance. To protect our children and thwart the state's efforts, our strategic actions should focus on four categories: teaching, avoiding, building, and organizing.

Teach

Our opportunity as parents is to nurture our children into becoming part of the resistance against the omnipotent state. This doesn't mean donning armor and heading into battle; sometimes, the greatest threats to an imperial force are insurgencies and guerrilla tactics, hiding in the shadows—acting when least expected. Resistance isn't just negative conflict—it's positive action creating the world we want to see. Casting that vision and helping our children pursue it requires teaching them about how and why our ideal world is threatened by an omnipotent state. Among the strategies you might include in this category, consider the following:

- **Demonstrate and encourage critical thinking.** Be skeptical about what you read in the news, especially from government sources, and share your skepticism and thought process with your children. Debate issues together. Learn about logical fallacies together—especially appeals to authority and why they're a problem. Challenge your children's opinions (ask them why they think what they think) and encourage them to back up what they say with evidence or logic. Encourage them to ask questions and resist the temptation to ever answer with "because I said so" or a similarly dismissive response. Involve them in conversations about "adult" issues with your spouse, siblings, or other peers.

- **Disconnect legality and morality.** Children are often raised to equate what's bad with whatever is illegal. When a young person's moral code is derived from laws made by politicians, they can too easily become blind followers willing to ignore their conscience and delegate their thinking to others. Instead, teach your children historical examples of when laws sanctioned horrible things like the Holocaust, slavery, segregation, and more—or when laws criminalized good things like hiding Jews from Nazis, helping runaway slaves, or protesting racist laws. Strengthen your children's internal moral compass by helping them understand the difference between what's *malum in se* (things that are bad in and of themselves, like theft or assault or murder) and *malum prohibitum* (things that are bad only because they are declared to be so, like jaywalking or having backyard chickens without a permit) so that they don't derive their sense of what's right and wrong from the state.

- **Identify objective truths.** In a culture that promotes "speaking your truth," there is a serious risk of substituting subjective opinions for objective facts. People who embrace this mindset focus more on personal perspective than on reality; in truth, they perceive that reality is what they feel and think, not what actually *is*. Those who insist on speaking "their" truth assume that they are their own source of truth and authority and, consequently, that no one else has the right to correct them—for they would only be speaking "their" truth to which they are equally entitled. It is the erasure of common norms, plain definitions, and a shared reality. This creates confusion, societal division, and weakens family bonds. Of course, there is either truth or untruth; there is one reality with objective facts. Our children need to recognize and resist this abandonment of objectivity so that they can make better informed and realistic decisions for their lives, grounded in evidence and logic.

- **Learn from—not merely about—history.** Those who fail to do so are more likely to repeat mistakes of the past, which is why the state dumbs down its curriculum and prefers civic illiteracy. "The most effective way to destroy people," an anonymous quote says, "is to deny and obliterate their own understanding of history." To create a better future, we need to learn from the past, which is why studying history as a family is critical. Understand, however, that most history textbooks focus on superficial factoids instead of substantive ideas we can learn from—and, worse, they often excuse the state's actions and downplay its atrocities. These are the very things we should be learning deeply about to understand just how dangerous the omnipotent state is to our liberty and how families historically have been threatened—often fatally so—by its actions. Try to find material that shares stories of the past in a way that makes them relatable to our modern day so we can be not only informed but also empowered to make better choices in our lives. This is the basis of our *America's History* series with the Tuttle Twins.

- **Be the change you wish to see in the world.** Fighting for a better world requires each of us to be eagerly engaged in a good cause (or two or five). We should demonstrate our commitment to our values through words *and* action, showing our children that having beliefs and thinking things isn't enough. A resistance without action is merely an intellectual exercise languishing in theory and dreams. We can't sit around thinking "someone ought to do something!" That teaches our children that we aren't actually committed to our ideas and are passive creatures reacting to others instead of actively trying to shape our world for the better. Just as surfing can't be taught in textbooks, becoming part of the resistance is something learned through experience—involving your children in activism projects, attending rallies, hosting book clubs, exploring entrepreneurial ventures, volunteering for service projects, and more. Let them learn by observing your behavior instead of merely listening to your lectures.

Avoid

Direct confrontation with the enemy can be dangerous; sometimes, a resistance flourishes best by avoiding conflict and instead concentrating energy on activities that have an indirect impact on undermining the strength and success of the enemy. Families could consider one or more of the following strategies to avoid the omnipotent state's influence in our lives:

- **Unplug from the Matrix.** In this fictional story, humans are controlled because their minds are plugged into the machines' system, paralyzing them into inaction because they don't understand that the things they believe to be real are actually false. In our world, we too often willingly plug ourselves into the state's media machinery, consuming content that confuses us about what is true. Important stories are ignored, unimportant drama is broadcast incessantly, problems are blamed on anything and everyone other than their actual causes, and those in power are rarely challenged. Journalism is largely dead; corporate media don't speak truth to power—they are a propaganda arm speaking the state's message to the masses. Media outlets routinely employ former government officials in a revolving door of corruption that almost never sees the state attacked. Rare acts of actual journalism, like the WikiLeaks exposé of the American government committing war crimes, are often punished—in this example, leading to an outright attack on Julian Assange. (The state wanted to send a message, and it was received loud and clear.) Edward Bernays wrote over a century ago of those who "pull the wires which control the public mind."[25] Refuse to give these thought controllers power over you by disconnecting yourself from their daily transmissions. Turn off the TV, ignore the "talking heads" on corporate media programs, be very skeptical of what you read on social media and from government spokespeople, and gain different perspectives on current events by reviewing commentaries from international publications and independent journalists. Don't trust but do verify.

- **Act as if free.** Henry David Thoreau's *Walden* chronicles the author's social experiment at Walden Pond, escaping what he called over-civilization in search of the "raw" and "savage delight" of the wilderness. One year into his two-year plan, the local tax collector confronted Thoreau and asked him to pay six years of delinquent poll taxes. Thoreau refused due to his opposition to the Mexican-American War and slavery and was subsequently incarcerated. His single-night jail stay, the result of a relative paying his "debt" to the state to free him (over his objections), prompted him to write *Civil Disobedience*, an influential essay that explores the interaction between man and the state. Freed from jail, children in the nearby area asked Thoreau to hunt for huckleberries with them. It was one of his favorite pastimes. One might imagine Thoreau breathing in deeply, standing on one of Concord's highest hills, as he looked around and observed, as he later wrote that "the state was nowhere to be seen."[26] Some are so intoxicated by the state—its promises, programs, and pageantry—that they could never fathom being so disconnected as Thoreau sought to become. They are "so completely within the institution" of the state, he wrote, that they "never distinctly and nakedly behold it." Like Thoreau, we should live our lives, to some extent, as if the state was not present—acting as if we were actually free. Build a shed in your yard without permission. Buy items directly from others to avoid sales taxes. Take home-cooked meals to neighbors without following commercial kitchen regulations. Explore cryptocurrencies, VPNs, and other tools to protect your privacy and keep the state's prying eyes at bay. In short, to the extent possible and reasonable, live your life on your terms as if you were independent and did not need the permission of others.

- **Flee the state's schools.** In the words of one pastor, "We cannot continue to send our children to Caesar for their education and be surprised when they come home as Romans."[27] In a political and economic context, we who desire freedom cannot surrender our impressionable children during their most intellectually formative years to the state's seminaries of propaganda and be surprised when they come home ignorant of the state's past atrocities and supportive of its present programs and policies. Government schools (including most charter schools) will not produce children that are skeptical of and resistant to the government. An independent family must avoid these institutions despite the allure of the supposedly "free" services they offer; sometimes, it is the free stuff that costs us the most. Whether parents elect to educate their children at home or in a co-op, micro school, private school, or via another alternative, avoiding the state's indoctrination system is critical.

Build

When Thomas Paine's *Common Sense* was first published, it was done anonymously because of its treasonous content. Some suspected that John Adams was the author, and he initially felt flattered. But the more he thought about the document, the less he liked it. Writing to his wife Abigail in 1776, Adams commented that Paine was "a better hand at pulling down than building."[28] A decade later, in a changed world, Adams reiterated this assessment as he surveyed the political landscape. "It is much easier to pull down a government, in such a conjuncture of affairs as we have seen, than to build up at such season as present."[29] A few short years later, on the issue of the unstable French Revolution, he opined in similar fashion: "Everything will be pulled down. So much seems certain. But what will be built up?"[30] To be successful in the long term, a resistance must have well-thought-out ideas on what can be edified in place of what is eliminated. To compete against the state, we need strong family units and robust mediating institutions in civil society. We who fight for freedom must be builders.

- **Systematize problem solving.** Life is full of problems, and too often, it's tempting to blame others and think, *Someone ought to do something!* This is why the state is so successful—though it is a societal disease, it masquerades as a cure; people look to politicians and their programs for salvation from their life's discomforts and challenges. Instead, they should identify ways that they can be the solution to their own problem, with support as needed from family and friends. Chances are, they were not raised to think this way—and parents who regularly swoop in to fix a child's problem can sometimes make matters worse because this conditions the child to look to authority figures and external sources for solutions to their problems. We can build up the resistance's rising generation to become problem solvers by approaching our children's challenges with a five-step sequence that, when repeated, will help them develop a second-nature approach to addressing their problems themselves. First, we should encourage our kids to vocally identify the problem— focusing on the root concern in a succinct way. This can help bring clarity to what actually troubles them and encourage introspection. Second, we should encourage brainstorming three to five possible solutions—even ones that might be silly or far-fetched. Third, have them create a pros/cons list so they can assess the merits of each idea and develop critical thinking skills as they evaluate their own suggestions. Fourth, having listed the possible positive and negative outcomes, they need to pick a solution and implement it. And, finally, you should help them review the results, compare what actually happened to what they thought would happen, and learn something from the experience that might apply to future problem solving. Repeating a process like this will help our children methodically identify ways that they can be the change they wish to see in the world.

- **Encourage entrepreneurship.** Building on their budding problem-solving skills, parents should prompt children of all ages to be producers (instead of moochers) by exposing them to entrepreneurial opportunities. Whether this is something as simple as a regular lemonade stand on the side of the road, a more serious effort through something like the Children's Entrepreneur Market or Children's Business Fair, an e-commerce business, or a home-based enterprise like lawn mowing, babysitting, baking, or another service for those in your community, we should provide our children with ongoing opportunities to create value for others. This strengthens our communities, develops relationships, and helps your children see the reward that comes (financially and otherwise) from serving others through the market. By profiting from problem solving, they will see that life is better when we voluntarily exchange our time and labor instead of lazily depending on a dole for survival.

- **Create projects.** Whether it's an informal group, a formal non-profit, or another structure, unite your family around a project that can serve as a vehicle for children to learn responsibility, service, planning, project management, marketing, fundraising, and more. By focusing on a structured set of activities through an organization, your children will be able to interact with others on a regular basis around a set of shared goals. They will see that success comes through collaboration with others instead of doing things on their own. And they will be able to help and be helped by others consistently as your family and others you rope in to help work together in pursuit of your organization's objective. Especially if the project is charitable in nature, this will give your children an outlet through which to problem solve on behalf of others, leading to increased humility, gratitude, and maturity. They will see that they can create solutions not just to their own problems but to others' problems as well—and that, in the aggregate, all of us working to help those around us is what creates a healthy society.

Organize

When angry colonists wanted to mount a resistance to the world's greatest superpower occupying their communities with soldiers, many of them formed a group called the Sons of Liberty to coordinate their civil disobedience, protest the British, and fight back. Their members included people like Samuel Adams, John Hancock, Paul Revere, Benedict Arnold, Patrick Henry, and many more. Their strategic defiance not only helped spark the Revolutionary War but also created an American tradition of grassroots activism that many organizations have since used to fight for the change they wished to see. Our resistance against the state similarly needs strategy, coordination, and a cohesive identity; we need to organize our efforts to succeed.

- **Create or adopt an identity.** The Sons of Liberty's success was partly due to their marketing efforts to get others talking about their defiant acts. Having a recognizable and reputable name got people talking about them. Their members shared an identity and felt they were "part of something." Humans crave identity and too often find it in the state as "citizens," like tribal fans of the local sports team. Instead, we should find other identities to affiliate and associate with. This could be religious, political, or cultural in nature. Your organization might be Floridians for Low Taxes, Kid Entrepreneurs, or Teen Changemakers. Modern groups like Moms for Liberty, Americans for Prosperity, Black Lives Matter, the Sierra Club, and countless other groups offer identity to their members and rally them to their cause. These can become the modern fraternal organizations de Tocqueville observed so approvingly, and they can be the means through which we can help others in need, so they don't turn to the state for help.

- **Get social.** "Neither do men light a candle, and put it under a bushel," Jesus said, "but on a candlestick; and it giveth light unto all that are in the house."[31] The ideas your family values and fights for shouldn't be confined to the walls of your home. As we build organizations and create projects to make a better world, we need to openly share our actions with others. Perhaps they will join or support us or simply be inspired by our actions and find similar opportunities in their own life. Too many people feel isolated despite how connected we are via social media, so our online advocacy should always invite others to join our cause, connect with us, and create relationships that will help enrich their lives and empower them in their journey. And we should cultivate new offline relationships through dinner or social parties, church or community service, and other outreach to those around us. It is these relationships that will create a stronger social fabric and help our children and their peers find strength and support from one another rather than seeking a handout from the state.

- **Circle the wagons.** Part of organizing is having a support system to rely on when attacked—and those who are successful will certainly have a target on their backs, whether it's persecution, so-called cancellation, or worse. When attacks would come on the frontier during a westward trek, pioneers would move their wagon train into a circle to provide cover. This defensive posture made it harder for an attack to succeed and also enabled them to better make offensive strikes with their firearms, shielded behind the wagon for protection. As we organize together in our resistance to the state, we can build our own social safety net to have the support of others when we face attacks for speaking out and standing up for truth.

- **Tell the truth.** Those who learn the truth have a duty to share it with others. That's what sixteen-year-old Helmuth Hübener felt when illegally listening to his brother's radio during the rise of Hitler's regime. The BBC transmissions told a different story from what the Nazis were saying, and so he began composing various anti-war and anti-Nazi leaflets, producing copies to share widely. "German boys! Do you know the country without freedom, the country of terror and tyranny?" he wrote in one of them. "Yes, you know it well, but are afraid to talk about it. They have intimidated you to such an extent that you don't dare talk for fear of reprisals. Yes you are right; it is Germany—Hitler Germany! Through their unscrupulous terror tactics against young and old, men and women, they have succeeded in making you spineless puppets to do their bidding." The leaflets were pinned on bulletin boards, stuffed into mailboxes, and inserted surreptitiously into people's coat pockets. As Helmuth learned,[32] truth is treason in an empire of lies. The state prefers "journalists" and citizens who will repeat its talking points and not question its actions; independent thinkers are a threat to those in power. As we organize strong families and mediating institutions to strengthen society and shrink the state, we need to speak openly and honestly about the corruption and destructive nature of our enemy.

STRENGTH IN NUMBERS

In the Bible, the prophet Elisha was under siege by a host of Syrian soldiers who wanted to neutralize the advantage he had been giving Israel's army by revealing to them the Syrians' plans. As they "compassed the city both with horses and chariots," Elisha's servant grew very worried. "Alas, my master!" he fretted. "How shall we do?" Elisha replied: "Fear not: for they that be with us are more than they that be with them." One can imagine the servant looking around at the clear imbalance between the Syrian army and the meager defensive forces, if any, that protected Elisha's community. But Elisha had a different perception—one that he asked God to share with the servant. So "the Lord opened the eyes of the young man; and he saw: and, behold, the mountain was full of horses and chariots of fire round about Elisha."[33] The servant now realized he was surrounded and supported by others who could help; he surely felt strength in numbers and more confident about his situation with that new insight.

We also can find strength in numbers. Despite being so disconnected, there are many of us who cherish freedom and want to protect our children from the sinister motives of the state—who understand history and see its mistakes repeating all around us today. But many of our would-be resistance feel isolated and alone, feeling like they're under constant ideological assault by people around them who don't share and often attack their core values. We need to find and connect with one another to create support systems and social networks of our own—not just online but in person also. Through connection, we can collaborate and share ideas, resources, and strategies to raise our children to thrive in today's world. United we stand, divided we fall. (Or, to quote *Lost*… live together, die alone.) This unity and strong social fabric are precisely what authoritarians despise, for it complicates their ability to shape society as they please—and it's why the state's strategy is to divide and conquer.

The Latin *divide et impera* ("divide to rule") has long been a strategy employed by conquerors to subjugate others, from Babylon and Macedonia to Gaul, Israel, and more societies throughout history. Sun Tzu wrote that "The control of a large force is the same principle as the control of a few men: it is merely a question of dividing up their numbers."[34] Niccolò Machiavelli, the Italian philosopher, similarly noted that a successful military strategist "ought to strive with all his skill to divide the forces of the enemy."[35] And as Marxism showed, this isn't just a battlefield tactic to exert physical dominance over an armed force—it's a political tool for aspiring authoritarians to amass power by pitting the public against one another. For Marx and his adherents, theirs was "a struggle of class against class, a struggle which, brought to its highest expression, means a complete revolution."[36] Dividing society into classes pits them against one another as smaller groups, rendering each side less able to oppose what is imposed on them by the state. In modern society, these divisions cross racial, gender, religious, ethnic, economic, and political lines. This serial segregation creates a constant search for victims in every subunit of society who are encouraged to seek retribution and reparations for their perceived problems. The "other side" are oppressors who are always painted as the enemy—not as rational individuals who are not responsible for the decisions of their ancestors or others in their "group." The state and its functionaries thus distract the populace with an endless series of silly squabbles that create contention and erode trust. Consequently, it is a very effective way of separating society into factions and ensuring that the people don't band together to resist their common oppressor, the state. Pitting us against one another makes it easier to pull us apart.

Put simply, the state thrives in an atomized society full of disconnected individuals. And while the family institution is best positioned to shield and support our children, it is increasingly in decline. What once was a tightly knit cluster of siblings and relatives creating and strengthening social fabric "has been crumbling in slow motion for decades,"[37] fragmented into divorced and single-parent families, with fewer children and relatives around to help. Intact families are still breaking, but differently; for example, where families once listened to their elders tell the family stories, now individuals sit around the TV or, with their own devices, watch *other* families' stories. For far too many families, home is a common residence and traffic control center—and not much more.

What we must realize, and quickly, is that we need each other. Like Frodo on his quest to throw the One Ring into Mount Doom or Harry

Potter relying on the help of Hermione, Ron, and countless others to fend off the foes they encountered, each hero's journey in life is truly a team effort. Martin Niemöller learned this lesson the hard way. As a Lutheran pastor in Germany, he initially sympathized with many ideas promoted by the Nazi party. But when Hitler rose to power in 1933, Niemöller became an outspoken critic of his interference in the church and, as a result, spent years in prisons and concentration camps. After the war, he lectured in various parts of Allied-occupied Germany, publicly repenting of "his inaction and indifference to the fate of many of the Nazis' victims."[38] He had stood by while the Nazis first targeted members of opposing political movements, which he turned a blind eye to since he disagreed with their politics. And more broadly, Niemöller felt that Germans—and especially the leaders of the various churches—bore some of the blame for Hitler's atrocities because of their silence surrounding the imprisonment, persecution, and execution of millions of people. It was during these lectures that he shared the views that were consolidated into this well-known quote:

> First they came for the socialists, and I did not speak out—because I was not a socialist.
>
> Then they came for the trade unionists, and I did not speak out—because I was not a trade unionist.
>
> Then they came for the Jews, and I did not speak out—because I was not a Jew.
>
> Then they came for me—and there was no one left to speak for me.[39]

As society increasingly polarizes[40] and people retreat to their tribes, we encourage the very atomization that most threatens our children. Divided into our subgroups, we find ourselves increasingly pitted against one another by propagandists and politicians seeking power. We fight against those we should be fighting *with*, failing to realize we have a common enemy—the very institution cheering on and benefitting from our conflict. Because the resistance needs strength, and strength comes in numbers, families should actively foster unity with anyone interested in creating a stronger social fabric that will benefit them and others. And although the family is the first line of resistance against the totalitarian state, it is not singularly responsible for shouldering this burden. To succeed, it needs—we need—the support of churches, civic institutions, community groups, schools, journalists, activists, philanthropists, researchers, writers, marketers, entrepreneurs, and countless other mediating institutions and individuals. Just as our bodies fight infection through a multilayered approach of resistance mechanisms, our children will thrive best when the efforts of their parents are augmented through the supportive actions of others.

If, as the saying goes, it takes a village to raise a child, then it takes everyone in the village to help protect the child from the roaming bandits and corrupt village leaders.

CONCLUSION

O N OCTOBER 23, 1956, A GROUP of university students organized a protest at the Hungarian Parliament Building to oppose the Soviet infiltration and domination of their country. Their ranks swelled with fellow Hungarians, and over 20,000 people united in chanting the National Song that the Soviets banned. "This we swear, this we swear, that we will no longer be slaves." They toppled Stalin's nearby statue, which had been erected on the site of a church demolished by the state, and erected a Hungarian flag in its place.

Meanwhile, some students had taken control of the local radio station and broadcasted their demands for political and economic reform. They were captured, and in the ensuing effort to secure their release, several students were shot by the police. The conflict erupted as more unarmed civilians were gunned down by Soviet troops and Hungarian security forces doing their bidding. Thus began a revolution.

As Red Army tanks descended on Budapest, civilians and defecting soldiers joined together in an armed uprising against the Soviet-controlled government. They fought off tanks with small arms and Molotov cocktails with great courage and surprising success. Many of the fighters were young men and young women with no military training, often mere teenagers, whose energy and agility outmaneuvered the Red Army. Others set about destroying communist monuments and burning communist literature, vandalizing Russian stores with the message *Ruszkik haza!* (Russians, go home!). Workers across the country began striking, grinding the economy to a halt. A new government was created, and around 8,000 political prisoners were released. Many Hungarians were euphoric, hoping for a brighter day as they suddenly found themselves freed from the oppression of their ruthless Soviet masters. Photos of elated, plainclothes civilians standing atop tanks holding weapons shocked the world.

Though the Soviet military was repelled and self-government secured, this was to be only a fleeting victory. Just a few days after they had left, the Soviets returned in far greater numbers. As part of what they called "Operation Whirlwind," the USSR's military completely encircled Budapest with thousands of tanks that were larger and stronger than the older ones that Hungarians had defeated, supplemented by around 200,000 foot soldiers who had instructions to "restore order" by shooting anyone who resisted. With such overwhelming firepower, the military regained control of their puppet state within a week; over 2,500 Hungarians died, and thousands more were wounded in the effort.[1]

After the resistance was crushed, some 200,000 Hungarians set out on foot across the border into Austria, seeking protection as refugees. One of the many families fleeing in pursuit of a better life for their children was the Hadjoks. Working their way in the bitter cold of mid-November across the final few miles of Hungarian soil, Mr. and Mrs. Hadjok were determined to escape the Soviet state to protect thirteen-year-old Vera and nine-year-old Johan. Finding freedom after crossing the bridge at Andau, an Austrian village near the border, the Hadjoks shared their fresh story with curious interviewers seeking to understand the situation. "Our whole family despised communism the moment it reached Hungary," Mr. Hadjok explained. He continued:

> Three times we tried to escape. In 1948, when little Johan was a baby, we tried to sneak into Yugoslavia, but we were caught. In 1949, when he could walk, we tried again, but again we were caught and punished... On the day the revolution broke we said to one another, "Now maybe we can have a decent nation," but when the Russians stormed back we agreed, "We will leave this cursed business." And we walked most of the way to Andau.[2]

Young Vera piled on, boldly telling the nearby adults that "Neither Russia nor the communists in Hungary could ever make us believe the lies they told us." Naturally, the interviewers were stunned by the boldness of this child. "How did you know they were lies?" one of them asked. Mrs. Hadjok answered:

> At night after we had put out the lights upstairs we would gather in the cellar, and I would teach the children the true history of Hungary. We would discuss morality and the Catholic religion... We never allowed the children to go to sleep until we had washed away the evil things they might have heard that day.[3]

The power of her words produced a reverent silence on the part of her supportive interrogators. Finally, someone asked, "Did all families do this?"

"I don't know," Mrs. Hadjok replied. "You see, we never knew who the [secret police] were in our community, and it would have been a great risk to tell even your best friend. But I think most families did it, in secret."[4]

Like so many under totalitarian rule, Hungarian families were terrified of the consequences of resistance. A simple statement from a child about something they read, or a parent's political opinion, could see Mom and Dad deported to Siberia, never to be seen again. Just like that, parents were paralyzed as their children were propagandized by the state, wondering at what age they could openly discuss the truth with their offspring. "You see," the family's interpreter explained, "this family had to judge the exact moment at which a boy could be saved from communism and yet not too soon for fear the child might inadvertently blurt out the truth and destroy the whole family."[5]

The curious onlookers were impressed with the family's strength, and particularly young Vera's impressive knowledge and passion. Mr. Hadjok made crystal clear how difficult it was to protect his children in such a state in which "the battle between school and parents never relaxed in an instant."[6]

> The communists had everything on their side. Candy, fruit, games, terror. We had only one thing, the lessons at night. The more the communists tried to destroy our family life, the more we taught family loyalty. It was like their pressing us down all day, in every way you could think of, but at night we grew up strongly again.[7]

This intentional de-indoctrination by Hungarian families paid off, for "when communist teachers lectured to such children," Mrs. Hadjok said, "The boys and girls knew what lies they were being told before the teacher stopped speaking."[8] Despite their trials—or perhaps precisely because of them—this family lived up to what Michael Novak described: "Between the omnipotent state and the naked individual looms the first line of resistance against totalitarianism: the economically and politically independent family, protecting the space within which free and independent individuals may receive the necessary years of nurture."[9]

It is possible that some will disregard the importance of this quote—and the supporting arguments provided in this book—on the basis that our experience is not that of the Hadjoks, their Hungarian countrymen, and countless others who have suffered under despotic regimes of decades past. Our modern society has moved past such totalitarianism, they might argue, and children are not under the same threats they once were. Of course, it is easy to rebut such fallacious thinking in light of myriad examples from modern society. Let's stick with Russia to start. A top Kremlin official recently told thousands of teachers in the country that "Ever since the fall of the Soviet Union, the Russian government's attempts at imparting a state ideology to schoolchildren have proven unsuccessful." In Russia's eyes, this is a failure. "We need to know how to infect them with our ideology," he said. "Our ideological work is aimed at changing consciousness."[10] This was echoed by another senior official at the conference who argued that "Patriotism should be the dominant value of our people." His definition of patriotism? "Readiness to give one's life for the Motherland."[11] And so the country is seeking a "wholesale reprogramming of Russian society" by rolling out new curriculum at its 40,000 government schools that extols Putin's accomplishments, venerates the state's military accomplishments, and encourages all children to join a new "youth movement" presided over by the president himself. If this sounds familiar, it should.

But these totalitarian tendencies are not reserved only for Russia and other countries with checkered histories of oppression and corruption. We in the so-called "land of the free" are likewise besieged by cultural, economic, and political forces that undermine the unity and strength of our families and encourage dependence upon the state. Paradoxically, it may be harder for us to resist these subtle, sinister efforts compared to the circumstances experienced by the Hadjok family. When confronted with oppression, many have the clear opportunity to fight or flee—to make a decision and act. The evil that boldly reveals itself causes great suffering, to be sure, but it also presents a direct confrontation that triggers a response. For example, an intruder in your home would prompt you to shoot in self-defense or run out the back door in search of safety. But when your attacker instead chooses more subtle means, such as slowly poisoning your home's water supply, what does your reaction look like? Perhaps because the state's actions are more "reasonable" and incremental than the open brutality of past regimes, we have all the more reason to be intentional and methodical about our resistance. If frogs die in pots of slowly boiling water, what does that say of us who live under governments that slowly restrict our rights?

History is clear that when the first line of resistance falls—when the family is weakened, either through internal decay or external pressure—the state fills the void and builds direct connections with atomized individuals. It is especially interested in our children, seeing in them the preservation and potential of its future power. And as the state grows in power and increasingly attracts the hearts and minds of our children, through heavy indoctrination on the one hand and the seductive lure of "free" handouts on the other, the need for the family becomes diminished. The solution to this vicious cycle is its inverse: a virtuous cycle where the stronger families become, the less we all need the state. As our families and communities rally together—providing the necessary nurture of the rising generation so we no longer throw our children into the state's open arms during their most formative years of intellectual development—the less we will need the state. As the population of people clamoring for its services and praising its programs declines, so too will its scope and size.

This need not be a bloody battle; our resistance against totalitarianism does not need to be confrontational to be successful. Just like many tyrannical restrictions in the past have been undermined through nonviolent civil disobedience and economic incentives, our own resistance can be peaceful. But more than that, it can be passive—a secondary byproduct of merely living our lives the way we ought to. We need not think of ourselves as equipping our children with proverbial swords and shields to fight the omnipotent state in a quixotic campaign for greatness. (As the Borg said, albeit in a much different context, resistance is futile.) Instead, we should act like the Hadjoks: creating unity and developing daily rituals to intentionally empower our children to learn truth, think critically, and act independently. In the dark, silent nights in Budapest, they didn't know whether other parents were acting similarly, "washing away the evil things" their children had been exposed to. But they *were*—and it was the children from these families that first actively resisted the Soviets in the streets and later found themselves on the same path to Andau to find freedom. As we each strengthen our families and nurture our children, we might find, as the Hadjoks and other Hungarians in the resistance did, that the aggregate impact of our individual efforts is profound. That is how we win in the long run—not by somehow finding strength to take on an omnipotent state but by weakening its foundations. Ultimately, the state's decline will be a natural byproduct of stronger families.

FOOTNOTES

INTRODUCTION

1. Alexis de Tocqueville, *Democracy in America, vol. II* (Cambridge: Sever and Francis, 1862), 392.
2. "The Best of Both Worlds, Part One," Star Trek: The Next Generation, Season 3, Episode 26, June 18, 1990.
3. *The Matrix*, directed by Andy Wachowski and Larry Wachowski (Warner Bros. Pictures, 1999).
4. Ibid.
5. Lois Lowry, *The Giver* (New York: Houghton Mifflin Harcourt, 1993), 193.
6. Ibid., 161-2.
7. Felix Salmon, "Gen Z Prefers 'Socialism' to 'Capitalism'," Axios, January 27, 2019, https://www.axios.com/socialism-capitalism-poll-generation-z-preference-1ffb8800-0ce5-4368-8a6f-de3b82662347.html.
8. de Tocqueville, *Democracy in America*.
9. Hanoverhenry, "Obama Website 'Life Of Julia' – Cradle To Grave Socialism For America," RedState, May 4, 2012, https://www.redstate.com/diary/hanoverhenry/2012/05/04/obama-website-life-of-julia-cradle-to-grave-socialism-for-america/.
10. "ED-HHS Policy on Family Engagement," U.S. Department of Education, accessed July 10, 2019, https://www2.ed.gov/about/inits/ed/earlylearning/families.html.

QUOTE

1. Michael Novak, *The Spirit of Democratic Capitalism* (Madison: New York, 1991), 165.

THE OMNIPOTENT STATE

1. J.R.R. Tolkien, *Tolkien: A Cultural Phenomenon* (Hampshire: Palgrave Macmillan, 2003), 178.
2. "MSNBC: We Have to Break Through This Idea 'That Kids Belong to Their Parents'," CNS News, April 8, 2013, https://www.cnsnews.com/news/article/msnbc-we-have-break-through-idea-kids-belong-their-parents.
3. "Bison by the Numbers," National Bison Association, https://bisoncentral.com/bison-by-the-numbers/.
4. *Warren v. District of Columbia*, 444 A.2d 1 (DC Ct. of Ap., 1981).
5. Ibid.
6. Fox News, "President Biden, first lady hosts the 2022 national and state teachers of the year," April 27, 2022, https://www.youtube.com/watch?v=JmoWVdmW1g0.
7. William L. Shirer, *Rise And Fall Of The Third Reich: A History of Nazi Germany* (New York: Simon & Schuster, 1990), 249.
8. Ibid.
9. Barbara Demick, *Nothing to Envy: Ordinary Lives in North Korea* (New York: Random House, 2009), 47.
10. Ibid., 120.
11. Andrei Lankov, "The Official Propaganda in the DPRK: Ideas and Methods," accessed July 27, 2020, http://community.fortunecity.ws/meltingpot/champion/65/propaganda_lankov.htm.
12. Karl Marx and Frederick Engels, *Manifesto of the Communist Party* (Chicago: Charles H. Kerr & Co., 1906), 39.
13. Anatoly Lunacharski, as quoted in *Marx and Education in Russia and China* (Abingdon: Routledge, 2012), 284. Lunacharski was a Marxist revolutionary the first Commissar of Education in the Soviet Union, responsible for the government-run education children.

14. See Kimberly Ells, *The Invincible Family* (Washington, DC: Regnery Publishing, 2020).

15. Jane Sneddon Little and Robert K. Triest, *Seismic Shifts: The Economic Impact of Demographic Change* (University of California, 2001), 57.

16. Wendy Z. Goldman, *Women, the State and Revolution: Soviet Family Policy and Social Life, 1917-1936* (Cambridge: Cambridge University Press, 1993), 333.

17. Ibid.

18. Adrian Lyttelton, *The Seizure of Power: Fascism in Italy, 1919-1929* (New York: Routledge, 2004), 223.

19. This policy was imposed in 1979, after a decade-long two-child policy that preceded it.

20. "The Legacy of China's One-Child Policy is an Aging Population," Radio Free Asia, December 19, 2019, https://www.rfa.org/english/news/china/legacy-12192019104145.html.

21. "Despite The End Of China's One-Child Policy, Births Are Still Lagging," NPR, July 16, 2018, https://www.npr.org/2018/07/16/629361870/despite-the-end-of-chinas-one-child-policy-births-are-still-lagging.

22. "The full heart-wrenching case of Alfie Evans and the journey that led his parents to a dramatic u-turn," *The Telegraph*, April 27, 2018, https://www.telegraph.co.uk/news/2018/04/26/tragic-case-alfie-evans-parents-wont-allowed-take-home-die/.

23. Alder Hey NHS Trust -v- Evans, [2018] EWHC 308 (Fam), accessed August 20, 2020, https://www.judiciary.uk/judgments/alder-hey-nhs-trust-v-evans/.

24. "Parents lose legal fight to keep Liverpool toddler on life support," *The Guardian*, February 20, 2018, https://www.theguardian.com/uk-news/2018/feb/20/parents-lose-legal-fight-keep-liverpool-toddler-life-support.

25. "Parents of Alfie Evans lose latest legal battle but vow to carry on against 'cruel bureaucracy'," *The Irish Post*, April 21, 2018, https://www.irishpost.com/news/parents-of-alfie-evans-lose-latest-legal-battle-but-vow-to-carry-on-against-cruel-bureaucracy-153687.

26. Murray Rothbard, *Anatomy of the State* (Auburn: Ludwig von Mises Institute, 2009), 11.

27. Otto Wenckstern, tr., *Goethe's Opinions on The World, Mankind, Literature, Science and Art* (London: John W. Parker and Son, 1853), 3.

28. Marx, *Manifesto*, 46.

29. Hannah Arendt, *Totalitarianism* (New York: Harcourt Brace Jovanovich, 1968), 168.

30. H.L. Mencken, "The Library," *The American Mercury, vol. 1* (University of California, 1924), 504.

31. Sean Sayers, *Plato's Republic: An Introduction* (Edinburgh University Press, 1999), 89.

32. Ibid., 90.

33. Morag Buchan, *Women in Plato's Political Theory* (New York: Routledge, 1999), 142.

34. Plato, as quoted in J.C. Davis, *Utopia and the Ideal Society: A Study of English Utopian Writing, 1516-1700* (London: Cambridge University Press), 40.

35. Further highlighting the connection between education and the state's desire to mold people, Horace Mann, the education reformer who pioneered the "common school" concept in the 1830s, once said, "Men are cast-iron, but children are wax." See Mary Tyler Peabody Mann, *The Life of Horace Mann* (Boston: Walker, Fuller & Company, 1865), 83.

36. 1 Samuel 8:19-20.

37. 1 Samuel 8:6.

38. 1 Samuel 8:11-20.

39. "The Terrifying Story of Hitler's Stolen Children," *The National Interest*, November 24, 2018, https://nationalinterest.org/blog/buzz/terrifying-story-hitler%E2%80%99s-stolen-children-36797.

40. Ibid.

41. "Kidnapping of children by Nazi Germany," Wikipedia, https://en.wikipedia.org/wiki/Kidnapping_of_children_by_Nazi_Germany.

42. "The Brutal History of Japan's 'Comfort Women'," History, July 21, 2019, https://www.history.com/news/comfort-women-japan-military-brothels-korea.

43. "Former comfort woman tells uncomforting story," DW, September 2, 2013, https://www.dw.com/en/former-comfort-woman-tells-uncomforting-story/a-17060384.

44. "Georgia family awarded $3.6M after SWAT team throws grenade at baby," Rolling Out, February 27, 2016, https://rollingout.com/2016/02/27/846658/.

45. "$3.6 Million Awarded In Flash-Bang Grenade Maiming Of Baby Bou," Cop Block, February 28, 2016, https://www.copblock.org/155092/3-6-million-settlement-reached-in-flash-bang-grenade-raid-maiming-of-baby-bou-bou/.

46. "Family of Toddler Injured by SWAT 'Grenade' Faces $1M in Medical Bills," ABC News, December 18, 2014, https://abcnews.go.com/US/family-toddler-injured-swat-grenade-faces-1m-medical/story.

47. "Court Rules Police Officer Who Shot 10-Year-Old Is Protected by Qualified Immunity," Reason, July 16, 2019, https://reason.com/2019/07/16/court-rules-police-officer-who-shot-10-year-old-is-protected-by-qualified-immunity/.

48. Marvin Ventrell, "The History of Child Welfare Law," *Child Welfare Law and Practice*, Case 117.

49. Vivek Sankaran, "Parens Patriae Run Amuck: The Child Welfare System's Disregard for the Constitutional Rights of Non-Offending Parents," Temp. L. Rev. 82, no. 1 (2009): 60.

50. *Prince v. Massachusetts*, 321 U.S. 158 (1944).

51. Stephen Hunt, "Parker Jensen's parents lose cancer case rights battle," *The Salt Lake Tribune*, March 30, 2011.

52. Ibid.

53. Ibid.

54. Milton Mayer, *They Thought They Were Free: The Germans, 1933-45* (Chicago: The University of Chicago Press, 1955), xix.

55. Ibid.

56. Oliver Thomson, *Mass Persuasion in History: An Historical Analysis of the Development of Propaganda Techniques* (Edinburgh: Paul Harris Publishing, 1977), 6.

57. Edward Bernays, *Propaganda* (Brooklyn: IG Publishing, 2005), 37.

58. Edward Bernays, *Biography of an Idea: The Founding Principles of Public Relations* (New York City: Simon and Schuster, 1965), 652.

59. Mayer, *They Thought*, 126.

60. Ibid., 166-172.

61. Ibid.

62. Ibid.

63. D.F. Lawson and K.T., et al., "Children can foster climate change concern among their parents," Nature Climate Change, 9, 458–462 (2019).

64. Ibid.

65. "Are public schools pushing a political agenda?," *The Standard*, August 8, 2019, https://www.thestandardsc.org/johnnelle-raines/is-your-childs-teacher-a-liberal-agenda-advocate.

66. "American Federation of Teachers President: 'We're Becoming More Political'," TownHall.com, August 6, 2018, https://townhall.com/tipsheet/briannaheldt/2018/08/06/american-federation-of-teachers-president-were-becoming-more-political-n2507335.

67. Woodrow Wilson, "Address Before the American Bar Association," *Selected Addresses and Public Papers of Woodrow Wilson* (New York: The Modern Library Publishers, 1918), 49.

68. "Professors and Politics: What the Research Says," Inside Higher Ed, February 27, 2017, https://www.insidehighered.com/news/2017/02/27/research-confirms-professors-lean-left-questions-assumptions-about-what-means.

69. During the COVID-19 lockdown when children had to access school services remotely, some teachers expressed concern that parents would be able to monitor, and thus frustrate, their propaganda efforts. For example, see "Philly Teacher: Parents With Access To Virtual Classrooms Would Do Damage To 'Honest Conversations About Gender/Sexuality'," Daily Wire, August 10, 2020, https://www.dailywire.com/news/philly-teacher-parents-with-access-to-virtual-classrooms-would-do-damage-to-honest-conversations-about-gender-sexuality.

70. Edward Bernays, *Crystallizing Public Opinion* (New York: Ig Publishing, 2011), 18.

71. Ibid., 31.

72. Ibid., 18.

73. Carl Resek, ed., *War and the Intellectuals: Collected Essays 1915–1919* (Indianapolis: Hackett Publishing Co., 1999), 84.

74. "America Has Been At War 93% of the Time – 222 Out of 239 Years – Since 1776," WashingtonsBlog.com, February 20, 2015, accessed August 10, 2019, https://washingtonsblog.com/2015/02/america-war-93-time-222-239-years-since-1776.html.

75. "America's Empire of Bases 2.0," *The Nation*, January 10, 2011, accessed May 2, 2011, https://www.thenation.com/article/americas-empire-bases-20/.

76. "Active Duty Military Personnel Strengths by Regional Area and by Country," U.S. Department of Defense, June 30, 2009, accessed August 2, 2019, http://www.globalsecurity.org/military/library/report/2009/hst0906.pdf.

77. "The Trillion-Dollar Defense Budget Is Already Here," The Independent Institute, March 15, 2007, accessed August 2, 2019, http://www.independent.org/news/article.asp?id=1941.

78. "U.S. Overseas Loans and Grants: Obligations and Loan Authorizations," U.S. Agency for International Development, http://www.census.gov/compendia/statab/2011/tables/11s1297.pdf.

79. Chris Hedges, *What Every Person Should Know About War* (New York: Free Press, 2003), 1.

80. Ibid.

81. Joe Glenton, "I fought in an unjust war. Let me tell you what that feels like," *The Guardian*, July 7, 2016, accessed August 15, 2019, https://www.theguardian.com/commentisfree/2016/jul/07/unjust-war-soldiers-iraq-afghanistan-vietnam.

82. Ibid.

83. "New veteran suicide numbers raise concerns among experts hoping for positive news," *Military Times*, October 9, 2019, https://www.militarytimes.com/news/pentagon-congress/2019/10/09/new-veteran-suicide-numbers-raise-concerns-among-experts-hoping-for-positive-news/.

84. See R. J. Rummel, *Death by Government* (New Brunswick: Transaction Publishers, 1994).

85. Lyndon Johnson, quoted in Tim McNeese and Richard Jensen, *Modern America: 1964–Present* (New York: Chelsea House, 2010), 27.

86. Richard Nixon, quoted in Kathleen Hall Jamieson, *Packaging the Presidency: A History and Criticism of Presidential Campaign Advertising* (New York: Oxford University Press, 1996), 241.

87. George W. Bush, quoted in Joe Klein, "It's Time For Extreme Peacekeeping," TIME, November 16, 2003, accessed August 2, 2019, http://content.time.com/time/nation/article/0,8599,543748,00.html.

88. Wake Forest University presidential debate, October 11, 2000, https://debates.org/voter-education/debate-transcripts/october-11-2000-debate-transcript/.

89. Carine Hajjar, "Life in Lebanon under Hyperinflation," Yahoo! News, July 31, 2020, https://news.yahoo.com/life-lebanon-under-hyperinflation-195352412.html.

90. Ibid.

91. "Zimbabwe villagers abandon land to dig for gold," Reliefweb, November 29, 2005, https://reliefweb.int/report/zimbabwe/zimbabwe-villagers-abandon-land-dig-gold.

92. Saifedean Ammous, *The Bitcoin Standard* (New Jersey: John Wiley & Sons, 2018), 94.

93. Lisa Quast, "Causes And Consequences Of The Increasing Numbers Of Women In The Workforce," *Forbes*, February 14, 2011, https://www.forbes.com/sites/lisaquast/2011/02/14/causes-and-consequences-of-the-increasing-numbers-of-women-in-the-workforce/?sh=25cc4772728c.

94. Kathryn Edin and Maria Kefalas, *Promises I Can Keep: Why Poor Women Put Motherhood before Marriage* (Los Angeles: University of California Press, 2007), 136

95. Joseph Chamie, "Out-of-Wedlock Births Rise Worldwide," YaleGlobal Online, March 16, 2017, https://yaleglobal.yale.edu/content/out-wedlock-births-rise-worldwide.

96. Apart Mathur, Hao Fu, and Peter Hansen, "The Mysterious and Alarming Rise of Single Parenthood in America," *The Atlantic*, September 3, 2013, https://www.theatlantic.com/business/archive/2013/09/the-mysterious-and-alarming-rise-of-single-parenthood-in-america/279203/.

97. Ammous, *Bitcoin Standard*, 95.

98. "The Story Behind Hanoi's Rat Massacre of 1902," Culture Trip, June 22, 2017, https://theculturetrip.com/asia/vietnam/articles/the-story-behind-hanois-rat-massacre-of-1902/.

99. Michael G. Vann, *White City on the Red River Race, Power, and Culture in French Colonial Hanoi, 1872-1954, vol. 1* (Santa Cruz: University of California, 1999), 154.

100. "Does it make sense to pay people to have kids?," BBC, October 22, 2019, https://www.bbc.com/worklife/article/20191017-does-it-make-sense-to-pay-people-to-have-kids.

101. Richard Thaler and Cass Sunstein, *Nudge: Improving Decisions About Health, Wealth, and Happiness* (New York: Penguin Group, 2008), 5.

102. David Pescovitz, "Cass Sunstein: Feds should 'cognitively infiltrate' online conspiracy groups," BoingBoing, https://boingboing.net/2010/02/08/case-sunstein-feds-s.html.

103. David Popenoe, *Disturbing the Nest: Family Change and Decline in Modern Societies* (New York: Aldine de Gruyter, 1988), 243.

104. Allowing the state to burden each individual directly is a precedent of sorts for its doing so with children, reducing the united front of parental and familial integrity and affecting each individual separately, including minors.

105. Popenoe, *Disturbing the Nest*, 148.

106. "135 000 hemmafruar sökes av singelmän," Dejting, December 3, 2009, accessed October 31, 2020, https://web.archive.org/web/20100530110034/http://www.expressen.se/dejting/1.1801333/135-000-hemmafruar-sokes-av-singelman.

107. "The Stigma of Being a Housewife," *The New York Times*, July 20, 2010, https://www.nytimes.com/2010/07/21/world/europe/21iht-LETTER.html.

108. Åsa Berglund, "The parental system in Sweden," Housewives: An comparison between Germany and Sweden, accessed October 31, 2020, https://sites.google.com/site/housewivesswedengermany/home.

109. Gwladys Fouché, "Where tax goes up to 60 per cent, and everybody's happy paying it," *The Guardian*, November 15, 2008, https://www.theguardian.com/money/2008/nov/16/sweden-tax-burden-welfare.

110. As quoted in "Sweden: No Model for Eastern Europe," FEE, November 1, 1990, https://fee.org/articles/sweden-no-model-for-eastern-europe/.

111. Robert Stein, "Taxes and the Family," *National Affairs*, Winter 2010, https://nationalaffairs.com/publications/detail/taxes-and-the-family.

112. Frédéric Bastiat, *The Bastiat Collection* (Auburn: Ludwig von Mises Institute, 2007), 308; modernized translation.

113. "In re Gault," Wikipedia, accessed March 20, 2021, https://en.wikipedia.org/wiki/In_re_Gault.

114. Anna Codrea-Rado, "Leave our kids alone: parents of free-range children bemoan 'land of snitches'," *The Guardian*, Marcy 4, 2015, https://www.theguardian.com/society/2015/mar/04/free-range-kids-movement-maryland-meitivs-child-neglect.

115. See "Vaccine Injury Compensation Data," Health Resources & Services Administration, accessed October 31, 2020, https://www.hrsa.gov/vaccine-compensation/data/index.html.

116. Lawrence A. Cremin, *The Transformation of the School: Progressivism in American Education, 1876-1957* (New York: Vintage Books, 1961), 10-11.

117. This was the state of Massachusetts, but the colony had previously passed the Old Deluder Satan Act in 1647 in an effort to cultivate Biblical literacy. The law, which later spread to other colonies, required towns of a certain size to fund and hire a teacher for the children in the area.

118. David T. Beito, *From Mutual Aid to the Welfare State: Fraternal Societies and Social Services, 1890-1967* (Chapel Hill: University of North Carolina Press, 2003), 19.

119. Marvin Olasky, *The Tragedy of American Compassion* (Washington, D.C.: Regnery Publishing, 1992), 150.

120. Dan Mitchell, "Does the War on Poverty Fight Destitution or Subsidize It?," International Liberty, accessed October 31, 2020, https://danieljmitchell.wordpress.com/2010/09/14/does-the-war-on-poverty-fight-destitution-or-subsidize-it/.

121. "Marriage license," Familypedia, accessed June 12, 2020, https://familypedia.wikia.org/wiki/Marriage_license.

122. "Maryland Enacts First Anti-Interracial Marriage Law," LegalFlip.com, accessed June 12, 2020, http://www.legalflip.com/ThisDayInTheLaw.aspx?id=271.

123. "Racial Integrity Laws (1924–1930)," Encyclopedia Virginia, accessed June 12, 2020, https://www.encyclopediavirginia.org/racial_integrity_laws_of_the_1920s.

124. "Marriage, History of," North Carolina History Project, accessed June 12, 2020, https://northcarolinahistory.org/encyclopedia/marriage-history-of/.

125. "Interracial Couple Denied Marriage License," NBC News, October 15, 2009, http://www.nbcnews.com/id/33332436/ns/us_news-life/t/interracial-couple-denied-marriage-license/.

126. "Civil & Human Rights Groups File Emergency Request to Inter-American Commission on Human Rights to Stop Family Separations, Reunite Families," Texas Civil Rights Project, May 31, 2018, https://texascivilrightsproject.org/civil-rights-groups-family-separations/.

THE NAKED INDIVIDUAL

1. Philips S. Foner, ed., *Frederick Douglass: Selected Speeches and Writings* (Chicago: Lawrence Hill Books, 1999), 367.

2. "Ebel Story," German American Internee Coalition, July 28, 2018, https://gaic.info/ebel-story/.

3. Ibid.

4. Catriona Kelly, *Children's World: Growing Up in Russia, 1890-1991* (New Haven: Yale University Press, 2007), 62.

5. Ibid.

6. Jennifer Keeley, *Life in the Hitler Youth* (San Diego: Lucent Books, 1999), 8–10.

7. William L. Shirer, *Rise And Fall Of The Third Reich: A History of Nazi Germany* (New York: Simon & Schuster, 1990), 249.

8. Radhey Shyam Chaurasi, *History of Western Thought* (New Dehli: Atlantic Publishers, 2001), 308.

9. "Are public schools pushing a political agenda?," *The Standard.*

10. *Democracy in America*, 392.

11. "Outrage as SWAT officers who disfigured toddler with grenade in botched drug raid will face NO charges," *Daily Mail*, October 7, 2014, https://www.dailymail.co.uk/news/article-2783268/Outrage-SWAT-officers-disfigured-toddler-botched-drug-raid-face-NO-charges.html.

12. "Transcript: White House Chief Of Staff John Kelly's Interview With NPR," NPR, May 11, 2018, https://www.npr.org/2018/05/11/610116389/transcript-white-house-chief-of-staff-john-kellys-interview-with-npr.

13. "US sees limitations on reuniting migrant families," Associated Press, February 2, 2019, https://apnews.com/article/48210bbf243e423ea151ff04e4878ce6.

14. "Texas sheriff defends raid on YFZ Ranch in one-on-one interview with Deseret News," *Deseret News*, June 3, 2008, https://www.deseret.com/2008/6/3/20256202/texas-sheriff-defends-raid-on-yfz-ranch-in-one-on-one-interview-with-deseret-news.

15. "Did Rozita Swinton's call set off the FLDS raid?," *Newsweek*, July 25, 2008, https://www.newsweek.com/did-rozita-swintons-call-set-flds-raid-93057.

16. "Comptroller Strayhorn Statement On Foster Care Abuse," Texas Comptroller, June 23, 2006, accessed August 4, 2021, https://web.archive.org/web/20110220151859/http://www.window.state.tx.us/news/60623statement.html.

17. Ibid.

18. Democide is the killing of a person by their own government.

19. 'I knew in my soul I had become a murderer'," *Daily Mail*, February 7, 2020, https://www.dailymail.co.uk/news/article-7977569/Ex-drone-operator-tells-dropped-missile-child-superiors-claimed-dog.html.

20. "Death From Above," *The Sun*, February 6, 2020, https://www.thesun.co.uk/news/10789432/drone-operator-brandon-bryant-killed-13-people-child-dog/.

21. "Where Is Outcry Over Children Killed by U.S.-Led Forces?," *Scientific American*, September 10, 2015, https://blogs.scientificamerican.com/cross-check/where-is-outcry-over-children-killed-by-u-s-led-forces/.

22. Ibid.

23. I do not use this word flippantly. A slave is someone who is compelled to render service to another person under threat of punishment for refusal. This is precisely the circumstance with a military draft.

24. "Constitution of the People's Republic of China," The National People's Congress of the People's Republic of China, accessed July 18, 2021, http://

www.npc.gov.cn/englishnpc/constitution2019/201911/1f65146fb6104dd3a2
793875d19b5b29.shtml.

25. "Emergency (Essential Powers) Act," Chapter 90, Section 2, March 25, 1992, https://sso.agc.gov.sg/SL/EEPA1964-RG8.

26. "Why we refused conscription into the Israeli Defence Force," PoliticsWeb, October 11, 2009, https://www.politicsweb.co.za/politics/why-we-refused-conscription-into-the-israeli-defen.

27. Ayn Rand, *Anthem* (Amazon, 2021), 34.

28. Aldous Huxley, *Brave New World* (New York: Harper Perennial, 2006), 5.

29. Lois Lowry, *The Giver* (Boston: Houghton Mifflin Harcourt, 2014), 27.

30. As quoted in *The New Yorker*, vol. 50 part 6, 1974.

31. Christopher Klein, "Stockholm Syndrome: The True Story of Hostages Loyal to Their Captor," History.com, April 9, 2019, https://www.history.com/news/stockholm-syndrome.

32. "The Stockholm Case," *Encyclopedia of Murder and Violent Crime* (Thousand Oaks: SAGE Publications, 2003), 453

33. See "Patty Hearst," Wikipedia, accessed August 20, 2022, https://en.wikipedia.org/wiki/Patty_Hearst.

34. Ibid.

35. Ibid.

36. Adrian Lyttelton, *The Seizure of Power: Fascism in Italy, 1919-1929* (New York: Routledge, 2004), 223.

37. David Livingstone Smith, *Less Than Human: Why We Demean, Enslave, and Exterminate Others* (New York: St. Martin's Press, 2011), 71.

38. Douglas Jehl and Andrea Elliott, "Cuba base sent its interrogators to Iraqi prison," *New York Times*, May 29, 2004.

39. *Fields v. Palmdale School District*, 427 F. 3d 1197.

40. *Prince v. Massachusetts*, 321 U.S. 158 (1944).

41. Erin O'Donnell, "The Risks of Homeschooling," *Harvard Magazine*, May–June 2020, https://harvardmagazine.com/2020/05/right-now-risks-homeschooling.

42. Elizabeth Bartholet, "Homeschooling: Parent Rights Absolutism vs. Child Rights to Education & Protection, *Arizona Law Review*, 62:1, https://arizonalaw- review.org/pdf/62-1/62arizlrev1.pdf.

43. Ibid.

44. Roger Soder, John I. Goodlad, and Timothy J. McMannon, eds., *Developing Democratic Character in the Young* (New York: Jossey-Bass, 2001), 164.

45. Ibid., 165.

46. Patrick Fagan and Robert Rector, "How Welfare Harms Kids," Heritage Foundation, June 5, 1996, https://www.heritage.org/welfare/report/how-welfare-harms-kids; see also "Family Welfare Cultures," *The Quarterly Journal of Economics*, vol. 129, no. 4, November 2014, https://doi.org/10.1093/qje/qju019.

47. Paul E. Peterson, "Government Should Subsidize, Not Tax, Marriage," *Education Next*, vol. 15, no. 2, https://www.educationnext.org/government-subsidize-not-tax-marriage/.

48. Robert Rector, "Married to the welfare state," Heritage Foundation, February 10, 2015, https://www.heritage.org/welfare/commentary/married-the-welfare-state.

49. W. Bradford Wilcox and Angela Rachidi, "Marriage, penalized: Does social-welfare policy affect family formation?," American Enterprise Institute, July 26, 2016, https://www.aei.org/research-products/report/marriage-penalized-does-social-welfare-policy-affect-family-formation/.

50. Alexis de Tocqueville, *Democracy in America, vol. 2* (Gutenberg.org), https://www.gutenberg.org/files/816/816-h/816-h.htm.

51. "Marcellus," in *Book of Saints* (1921), available on CatholicSaints.Info, Nov. 19, 2014, https://catholicsaints.info/book-of-saints-marcellus-30-october.

52. *Reynolds v. United States*, 98 U.S. 145 (1878).

53. "Text of Mayor Giuliani's Farewell Address," *The New York Times*, December 27, 2001, https://www.nytimes.com/2001/12/27/nyregion/text-of-mayor-giulianis -farewell-address.html.

54. Monica Stensland, *Habsburg Communication in the Dutch Revolt* (Amsterdam: Amsterdam University Press, 2012) 106.

55. William Anthony Hay, "The Loyalist Arguments," The Russell Kirk Center, June 30, 2019, https://kirkcenter.org/reviews/the-loyalist-arguments/.

56. *The Daily Dispatch*, July 6 1855, https://chroniclingamerica.loc.gov/lccn/sn84024738/1855-07-06/ed-1/seq-2/.

57. "The Fight to Define Romans 13," *The Atlantic*, June 15, 2018, https://www.theatlantic.com/ideas/archive/2018/06/romans-13/562916/.

58. "Why is Jeff Sessions quoting Romans 13 and why is the bible verse so often invoked?," *USA Today*, June 16, 2018, https://www.usatoday.com/story/news/2018/06/16/jeff-sessions-bible-romans-13-trump-immigration-policy/707749002/.

59. Bernays, *Propaganda*, 38.

60. "Gulag of the Mind: Why North Koreans Cry for Kim Jong-il," *The Atlantic*, December 22, 2011, https://www.theatlantic.com/international/archive/2011/12/gulag-of-the-mind-why-north-koreans-cry-for-kim-jong-il/250419/.

61. See, for example, William Craven, *Sermons on the Evidence of a Future State of Rewards and Punishments* (University of Cambridge, 1775).

62. de Tocqueville, *Democracy in America, vol. II*, 392.

63. Elder D. Todd Christofferson, "Moral Discipline," October 2009 General Conference of The Church of Jesus Christ of Latter-day Saints, https://www.churchofjesuschrist.org/study/general-conference/2009/10/moral-discipline.

64. The North Korea Constitution states that "religion must not be used as a pretext for drawing in foreign forces or for harming the State or social order." See "2020 Report on International Religious Freedom: Democratic People's Republic of Korea," U.S. Department of State, May 12, 2021, https://www.state.gov/reports/2020-report-on-international-religious-freedom/north-korea/.

65. Jean H. Lee, "How North Korean Children are Taught to Hate Americans," *Newsweek*, July 6, 2017, https://www.newsweek.com/how-north-korean-children-are-taught-hate-americans-632334

66. "North Korean Defector Exposes Life in North Korea," The Rubin Report, November 22, 2020, https://www.stitcher.com/show/the-rubin-report/episode/north-korean-defector-exposes-life-in-north-korea-yeonmi-park-interview-79609358.

67. Hannah Arendt, *Totalitarianism* (San Diego: Harvest, 1968), 172.

68. Bernays, *Propaganda*, 37.

69. Thaler and Sunstein, *Nudge*, 5.

70. Allen W. Dulles, "Brain Warfare," Central Intelligence Agency, https://www.cia.gov/readingroom/docs/CIA-RDP84-00161R000100150010-3.pdf.

71. Ibid.

72. "Project MKUltra, the CIA's Program of Research in Behavioral Modification," Joint Hearing before the Select Committee on Intelligence, August 3, 1977, 75.

73. Ibid., 74.

74. Dulles, "Brain Warfare."

75. "Project MKUltra," Joint Hearing, 83.

76. Christopher Bergland, "The Neuroscience of Trust," Psychology Today, August 12, 2015, https://www.psychologytoday.com/us/blog/the-athletes-way/201508/the-neuroscience-trust.

77. Roderick M. Kramer, "Rethinking Trust," *Harvard Business Review*, June 2009, https://hbr.org/2009/06/rethinking-trust.

78. See "Milgram experiment," Wikipedia, https://en.wikipedia.org/wiki/Milgram_experiment.

79. Following the attack on 9/11, President Bush and his associates insinuated that Saddam was somehow involved and that his weapons of mass destruction were linked to the event, hoping that the public ire over 9/11 would spill over into support for military intervention in Iraq, which many in the administration had long desired. Months into the war, a reporter backed the president into a corner on the issue, leading him to reply that "we've had no evidence that Saddam Hussein was involved" with the 9/11 attacks. Despite the later denial, many Americans continued to believe the initial lies.

80. Medications like Vioxx, Quaalude, Darvon & Darvocet, and many others were approved by the U.S. Food and Drug Administration before later being pulled from the market after killing tens of thousands of people.

81. Widespread obesity, diabetes, and chronic illness is heavily linked to diet, and the government's distortion of decision making in nutrition have caused myriad problems. For example, telling people to avoid fat prompted a wave of highly processed products marketed as "low fat," yet this junk food has caused a number of problems far worse. For more, see "The Government Has Been Meddling in Food and Nutrition for a Long Time," Foundation for Economic Education, November 27, 2017, https://fee.org/articles/the-government-has-been-meddling-in-food-and-nutrition-for-a-long-time/.

82. "Poll: Iraq war could wound GOP at polls," CNN, September 25, 2006, https://www.cnn.com/2006/POLITICS/09/06/iraq.poll/index.html.

83. Mann, *The Life of Horace Mann*, 83.

84. Thomson, *Mass Persuasion*, 6.

85. Shirer, *Rise And Fall Of The Third Reich*, 249.

86. Jo Ann Boydston, ed., *The Later Works of John Dewey, vol. 3* (Carbondale: Southern Illinois University Press, 2008), 230.

87. Ibid., 409.

88. William D. Gairdner, *The War Against the Family* (Toronto: Stoddart Publishing Co., 1992), 225.

89. Mencken, "The Library," 504.

90. The National Commission on Excellence in Education in 1983, after reviewing the country's school system and curricula, reported that "The educational foundations of our society are presently being eroded by a rising tide of mediocrity that threatens our very future as a nation and as a people." See "A Nation at Risk: The Imperative for Educational Reform," The National Commission on Excellence in Education, April 1983.

91. Resek, *War and the Intellectuals*, 84.

FAMILY INDEPENDENCE

1. Bertrand de Jouvenel, *On Power: The Natural History of Its Growth* (Indianapolis: Liberty Fund, 1993; original French edition 1945), 388–389.

2. Alberto Manguel, ed., *On Lying in Bed and Other Essays by G.K. Chesterton* (Calgary: Bayeux Arts, 2000), 154.

3. Utah Code 62A-4a-201(1)(d).

4. Ibid.

5. "Police Raid Home, Seize Children, of Homeschooling Family in Germany," *The Christian Post*, August 30, 2013, https://www.christianpost.com/news/police-raid-home-seize-children-of-homeschooling-family-in-germany.html.

6. Ibid.

7. Robert Clarke, "The German Government Forcibly Removed These Children From Their Parents Over Homeschooling," *The Daily Signal*, January 14, 2019, https://www.dailysignal.com/2019/01/14/the-german-government-forcibly-removed-these-children-from-their-parents-over-homeschooling/.

8. "European court rules against German homeschooling family," *Deutsche Welle*, January 10, 2019, https://www.dw.com/en/european-court-rules-against-german-homeschooling-family/a-47021333.

9. Ibid.

10. Christian Poole, "The Nazi Origins of Germany's Ban on Homeschooling," *ThinkingWest*, June 22, 2020, https://thinkingwest.com/2020/06/22/nazi-ban-homeschooling/.

11. "European court rules against German homeschooling family."

12. "European Human Rights Court Upholds Nazi Ban on Homeschooling," *The Brussels Journal*, September 28, 2006, https://www.brusselsjournal.com/node/1389.

13. "State Histories of Homeschooling," Coalition for Responsible Home Education, https://responsiblehomeschooling.org/research/histories/.

14. "Russia's Putin seeks to stimulate birth rate," BBC, January 15, 2020, https://www.bbc.com/news/world-europe-51120165.

15. "Birth rate up after baby bonus," *The Sydney Morning Herald*, September 16, 2006, https://www.smh.com.au/national/birth-rate-up-after-baby-bonus-20060916-gdoekm.html.

16. "In Estonia, paying women to have babies pays off," *The Wall Street Journal*, October 20, 2006, https://old.post-gazette.com/pg/06293/731744-82.stm.

17. "Baby bonus," Wikipedia, accessed December 1, 2021, https://en.wikipedia.org/wiki/Baby_bonus.

18. "When Governments Pay People To Have Babies," NPR, November 3, 2011, https://www.npr.org/sections/money/2011/11/03/141943008/when-governments-pay-people-to-have-babies.

19. Though the author could not source this quote, its essence is expounded upon at length in Thoreau's magnificent essay, *Civil Disobedience*.

20. Gilbert K. Chesterton, *Orthodoxy* (New York: John Lane & Co., 1909), 85.

21. Ibid.

22. See F.A. Hayek, *The Fatal Conceit* (University of Chicago Press, 1989).

23. "English Poor Laws," Economic History Association, accessed December 26, 2021, https://eh.net/encyclopedia/english-poor-laws/.

24. Benjamin Franklin, "On the Price of Corn and Management of the Poor, 1766," Founding.com, accessed December 26, 2021, https://founding.com/founders-library/american-political-figures/benjamin-franklin/on-the-price-of-corn-and-management-of-the-poor/.

25. Ibid.

26. Nicholas Eberstadt, "Are Entitlements Corrupting Us? Yes, American Character Is at Stake," *The Wall Street Journal*, August 31, 2012, https://www.wsj.com/articles/SB10000872396390444914904577619671931313542.

27. Ibid.

28. "Obama Is Going To Pay For My Gas And Mortgage!!!," YouTube, accessed December 28, 2021, https://www.youtube.com/watch?v=z8lXEY8O0tQ.

29. "The Free Obama Phone: Real or Urban Legend?," Free Government Cell Phones, accessed December 28, 2021, https://www.freegovernmentcellphones.net/faq/obama-phone.

30. "Original Obamaphone Lady: Obama Voter Says Vote for Obama because he gives a free Phone," YouTube, accessed December 28, 2021, https://www.youtube.com/watch?v=tpAOwJvTOio.

31. Loyd S. Pettegrew, "The High Cost of 'Free'," Mises Institute, June 5, 2013, https://mises.org/library/high-cost-free.

32. Paul E. Peterson, "Government Should Subsidize, Not Tax, Marriage," Education Next, accessed December 29, 2021, https://www.educationnext.org/government-subsidize-not-tax-marriage/.

33. Robert Rector, "Married to the welfare state," Heritage Foundation, February 10, 2015, https://www.heritage.org/welfare/commentary/married-the-welfare-state.

34. Robert Rector, "How Welfare Undermines Marriage and What to Do About It," Heritage Foundation, November 17, 2014, https://www.heritage.org/welfare/report/how-welfare-undermines-marriage-and-what-do-about-it.

35. Larry Schweikart, *Reagan: The American President* (New York: Post Hill Press, 2020), 41.

36. Richard Polenberg, *The Era of Franklin D. Roosevelt 1933-1945: A Brief History with Documents* (Boston: Bedford, 2000), 51.

37. W. Gibb Dyer, "Family matters: Why strong families make strong economies," *Deseret News*, November 11, 2014, https://www.deseret.com/2014/11/11/20552523/family-matters-why-strong-families-make-strong-economies.

38. To be hanged, drawn and quartered was the penalty in England for those convicted of high treason. Convicts were fastened to a wooden panel and drawn by horse to the place of execution, where they were hanged (almost to the point of death), disemboweled, beheaded, and quartered (chopped into four pieces). Their remains were often displayed in prominent places across the country, ostensibly as a warning to sympathetic rebels who would be treated the same if caught and convicted.

39. Thomas Paine, *The American Crisis* (London: R. Carlile, 1819), 63.

40. Daniel Di Martino, "Venezuela was my home, and socialism destroyed it. Slowly, it will destroy America, too.," *USA Today*, February 15, 2019, https://www.usatoday.com/story/opinion/voices/2019/02/15/donald-trump-venezuela-socialism-bernie-sanders-ilhan-omar-column/2861461002/.

41. Ibid.

42. See Robert Conquest, *The Harvest of Sorrow: Soviet Collectivization and the Terror-Famine* (Oxford: Oxford University Press, 1987).

43. See Frank Dikötter, *Mao's Great Famine: The History of China's Most Devastating Catastrophe, 1958-62* (London, Bloomsbury Paperbacks, 2010).

44. "A vivid account of the Chinese Revolution," *The Evening Standard*, August 22, 2013.

45. See Matthew White, *Atrocities: The 100 Deadliest Episodes in Human History* (New York: W. W. Norton & Company, 2011). Roughly 64 million people were killed in or because of combat in international and domestic wars.

46. F.A. Hayek, *The Fatal Conceit: The Errors of Socialism* (1988), 76.

47. Ibid., 27.

48. Virginia Postrel, *The Future and Its Enemies* (New York: Touchstone, 1999), 40.

49. Bill Bonner, "Why Central Planning Fails," *Daily Reckoning*, April 25, 2013, https://dailyreckoning.com/why-central-planning-fails/.

50. Thomas Blass, "The Man Who Shocked The World," Psychology Today, March 2002, https://www.psychologytoday.com/intl/articles/200203/the-man-who-shocked-the-world.

51. Bernays, *Propaganda*, 37.

52. Carmen Alexe, "I Grew Up in a Communist System. Here's What Americans Don't Understand About Freedom," Foundation for Economic Education, March 9, 2018, https://fee.org/articles/i-grew-up-in-a-communist-system-here-s-what-americans-don-t-understand-about-freedom/.

53. "Fourth Annual Report on U.S. Attitudes Toward Socialism," Victims of Communism Memorial Foundation.

54. C. S. Lewis, "Learning in War-Time," in *The Weight of Glory*, ed. Walter Hooper (San Francisco, CA: Harper San Francisco, 2001), 59.

55. Michael Federici, "The Politics of Prescription: Kirk's Fifth Canon of Conservative Thought," Intercollegiate Studies Institute, October 8, 2014, https://isi.org/intercollegiate-review/the-politics-of-prescription-kirks-fifth-canon-of-conservative-thought/.

56. Russell Kirk, "Ten Conservative Principles," The Russell Kirk Center, accessed February 6, 2022, https://kirkcenter.org/conservatism/ten-conservative-principles/.

57. Jack Birner and Rudy Van Zijp, eds., *Hayek, Coordination, and Evolution* (New York: Routledge, 1994), 257.

58. Anne Frank, *The Diary of Anne Frank* (New York: Doubleday, 2003), 563.

59. Alexa Lardieri, "Study: Many Americans Report Feeling Lonely, Younger Generations More So," *U.S. News and World Report*, May 1, 2018, https://www.usnews.com/news/health-care-news/articles/2018-05-01/study-many-americans-report-feeling-lonely-younger-generations-more-so.

60. Arendt, *Totalitarianism*, 172.

61. Steven Ruggles, "Multigenerational families in nineteenth-century America," *Continuity and Change* 18 (1), 2003, 139–165.

62. Ibid.

63. de Tocqueville, *Democracy*, 129–30.

64. Ibid.

65. Wenckstern, *Goethe's Opinions*, 3.

66. Arendt, *Totalitarianism*, 173.

67. David T. Beito, *From Mutual Aid to the Welfare State: Fraternal Societies and Social Services, 1890–1967* (Chapel Hill: University of North Carolina Press, 2003), 5.

68. Ibid., 28.

69. Ibid., 14.

70. Ibid., 20.

71. Ibid., 19.

72. Ibid., 231.

73. Jonathan Gruber and Daniel M. Hungerman, "Faith-based charity and crowd-out during the great depression," *Journal of Public Economics*, no. 91 (2007), 1.

74. Ibid.

75. Beito, *From Mutual Aid to the Welfare State*, 234.

NECESSARY NURTURE

1. "Supreme Court blocks Scottish Government's 'totalitarian' Named Person scheme in historic ruling," The Christian Institute, July 28, 2016, https://www.christian.org.uk/press_release/supreme-court-blocks-scottish-governments-totalitarian-named-person-scheme-in-historic-ruling/.

2. "New UN LGBT Expert Doubles Down Against Religious Freedom, Describes 'Entry Points' for Homosexual and Transgender Rights," Center for Family and Human Rights, February 2, 2017, https://c-fam.org/friday_fax/new-un-lgbt-expert-doubles-religious-freedom-describes-entry-points-homosexual-transgender-rights/.

3. "A Nation at Risk: The Imperative for Educational Reform," The National Commission on Excellence in Education, April 1983.

4. Ibid.

5. William T. Harris, *The Theory of Education* (Syracuse: C.W. Bardeen, 1893), 28-29.

6. Ibid., 30.

7. Johann Gottlieb Fichte, *Addresses to the German Nation* (Chicago: The Open Court Publishing Co., 1922), 22.

8. Ibid., 187.

9. Jo Ann Boydston, ed., *The Later Works of John Dewey, vol. 3* (Carbondale: Southern Illinois University Press, 2008), 230.

10. Sabrina Ramet, *Catholicism and Politics in Communist Societies* (Duke University Press), 232–3.

11. Based on campaign contribution data from the Federal Election Commission. See "Democratic vs. Republican Occupations," Verdant Labs, accessed March 3, 2022, http://verdantlabs.com/politics_of_professions/index.html.

12. Dana Goldstein, "American history textbooks can differ across the country, in ways that are shaded by partisan politics," *The New York Times*, January 12, 2020, https://www.nytimes.com/interactive/2020/01/12/us/texas-vs-california-history-textbooks.html.

13. Ibid.

14. George Orwell, "Politics and the English Language," The Orwell Foundation, accessed March 3, 2022, https://www.orwellfoundation.com/the-orwell-foundation/orwell/essays-and-other-works/politics-and-the-english-language/.

15. Emma Botelho, "The Direction of Dinner," *The Clarion*, https://lseclarion.com/12133/uncategorized/the-direction-of-dinner-as-family-dynamics-change-shared-dinnertime-doesnt-disappear-it-evolves/.

16. Jamie Ballard, "Most parents wish they were having family dinners more often," YouGov, November 12, 2019, https://today.yougov.com/topics/lifestyle/articles-reports/2019/11/12/family-dinner-poll-survey.

17. "Desires, Barriers and Directions for Shared Meals at Home," Food Marketing Institute Foundation, June 2017, https://www.fmi.org/docs/default-source/familymeals/fmi-power-of-family-meals-whitepaper-for-web.pdf.

18. James Clear, *Atomic Habits* (New York: Penguin, 2018), 276.

19. To start this process, consider subscribing to our podcast for families: "The Way the World Works: A Tuttle Twins Podcast." You can find it on your favorite podcast app, and each episode is around 15 minutes, making them easy to listen for busy families on the go.

20. "S.C. mom's arrest over daughter alone in park sparks debate," CBS News, July 28, 2014, https://www.cbsnews.com/news/south-carolina-moms-arrest-over-daughter-alone-in-park-sparks-debate/.

21. "Let Grow Legislative Toolkit," LetGrow.org, accessed August 20, 2022, https://letgrow.org/legislative-toolkit/ (text used with permission of the author).

22. Ibid.

23. Lenore Skenazy, "Mom Handcuffed, Jailed for Letting 14-Year-Old Babysit Kids During COVID-19," Reason, February 8, 2022, https://reason.com/2022/02/08/melissa-henderson-babysit-covid-arrest-blairsville/.

24. "'Let them be kids!' Is 'free-range' parenting the key to healthier, happier children?," *The Guardian*, August 16, 2021, https://www.theguardian.com/lifeandstyle/2021/aug/16/let-them-be-kids-is-free-range-parenting-the-key-to-healthier-happier-children.

25. "Have You Ever Wanted to Let Your Kids Do Something Independently — But Didn't, for Fear of Someone Calling 911?," Let Grow, accessed April 14, 2022, https://letgrow.org/have-you-ever-wanted-to-let-your-kids-do-something-independently-but-didnt-for-fear-of-someone-calling-911/.

26. "America Is Safer Than Ever, So Why Are Parents So Scared?," *The Huffington Post*, July 30, 2012, https://www.huffpost.com/entry/child-safety_b_1717100.

27. Letter to M. Mazzei, Minerva (New York: 1791).

28. For more on this, see my book *Passion-Driven Education: How to Use Your Child's Interests to Ignite a Lifelong Love of Learning.*

29. Katherine Peach, "What is the Anti-Work Movement?" Millennial Money, March 25, 2022, https://millennialmoney.com/anti-work-movement/.

30. Stephen Moore, "We've Become a Nation of Takers, Not Makers," *The Wall Street Journal*, April 1, 2011, https://www.wsj.com/articles/SB10001424052748704050204576219073867182108.

31. "Biden calls paying higher taxes a patriotic act," MSNBC, September 18, 2008, https://web.archive.org/web/20110301164311/http://www.msnbc.msn.com/id/26771716/ns/politics-decision_08/.

32. Liberty, safety, and Benjamin Franklin," *The Washington Post*, November 11, 2014, https://www.washingtonpost.com/news/volokh-conspiracy/wp/2014/11/11/liberty-safety-and-benjamin-franklin/.

33. John Locke, *Second Treatise on Government* (Gutenberg.org), https://www.gutenberg.org/files/7370/7370-h/7370-h.htm.

34. "Echo," *The Americans*, season 2, episode 13, May 21, 2014.

35. David L. Hoffman, *Stalinist Values: The Cultural Norms of Soviet Modernity, 1917–1941* (Ithaca: Cornell University Press, 2003), 107.

36. Ibid.

37. Locke, *Second Treatise.*

THE RESISTANCE

1. Heather Lehr Wagner, *Elie Wiesel, Messenger for Peace* (New York: Chelsea House, 2007), 96.

2. See "Salt March," Wikipedia, https://en.wikipedia.org/wiki/Salt_March.

3. Steven Ruggles, "Multigenerational families in nineteenth-century America," *Continuity and Change* 18 (1), 2003, 139–165.

4. *The Matrix*, directed by Andy Wachowski and Larry Wachowski (Warner Bros. Pictures, 1999).

5. "The 'Woke' Lancet Asks If It's Acceptable To Have Children," American Council on Science and Health, November 12, 2019, https://www.acsh.org/news/2019/11/12/woke-lancet-asks-if-its-acceptable-have-children-14395.

6. "Is it immoral to have babies in the era of climate change?," National Post, August 19, 2019, https://nationalpost.com/life/is-it-immoral-to-have-babies-in-the-era-of-climate-change.

7. Ibid.

8. "Americans are Having Fewer Babies. They Told Us Why.," *The New York Times*, July 5, 2018, https://www.nytimes.com/2018/07/05/upshot/americans-are-having-fewer-babies-they-told-us-why.html.

9. "The Coming Crisis: How Government Dependency Threatens America's Freedom," The Heritage Foundation, May 8, 2001, https://www.heritage.org/political-process/report/the-coming-crisis-how-government-dependency-threatens-americas-freedom.

10. 85% of U.S. parents send their child to public school. See "Parent Income, Degree, Religion Key Factors in School Choices," Gallup, August 28, 2017, https://news.gallup.com/poll/217247/school-choices-vary-parent-religion-education-income.aspx.

11. "74 percent say Americans too dependent on the government," Fox News, December 20, 2015, https://www.foxnews.com/politics/fox-news-poll-74-percent-say-americans-too-dependent-on-the-government.

12. "Dependency on Government Continues to Grow," *The New American*, December 13, 2011, https://thenewamerican.com/dependency-on-government-continues-to-grow/.

13. David Stanford Burr, *Ronald Reagan: Quotes and Quips* (New York: Wellfleet Press, 2015), 88.

14. Ayn Rand, *Atlas Shrugged* (New York: Signet, 1985), 957.

15. Georg Wilhelm Friedrich Hegel, *The Philosophy of History* (New York: Cosmo Classics, 2007), 6.

16. "Civic Illiteracy Fuels Misinformation," National Civic League, July 28, 2021, https://www.nationalcivicleague.org/civic-illiteracy-fuels-misinformation/.

17. Gore Vidal, *Imperial America: Reflections of the United States of Amnesia* (New York: Nation Books, 2004).

18. John P. Foley, ed., *The Jefferson Cyclopedia: A Comprehensive Collection of the Views of Thomas Jefferson* (New York: Funk & Wagnalls, 1900), 274.

19. Henry David Thoreau, *Walden* (New York: Thomas Y. Crowell & Co., 1910), 7.

20. The original quote's provenance is questionable, though often attributed to Henry Ford. See "Whether You Believe You Can Do a Thing or Not, You Are Right," Quote Investigator, accessed July 4, 2022, https://quoteinvestigator.com/2015/02/03/you-can/.

21. The Soviets used their Committee for State Security; East Germany had their "unofficial collaborators" under the control of the Ministry for State Security; Czechoslovakia had its "State Security," Poland their "Ministry of Public Security," and Hungary its "State Protection Authority"; the International and State Defense Police in Portugal used bufos (snitches) to empower their secret police.

22. Edward Livingston, as quoted in *House Reports, 74th Congress, 1st Session, vol. 4* (Washington: U.S. Government Printing Office, 1935), 7.

23. Sun Tzu, *The Art of War* (Standard Ebooks, 2002), 183.

24. Ibid., 35.

25. Bernays, *Propaganda*, 38.

26. Henry David Thoreau, *Civil Disobedience* (Salt Lake City: Libertas Institute, 2014), 24.

27. Voddie Baucham Jr., *Family Driven Faith* (Wheaton: Crossway, 2007), 202.

28. David McCullough, *John Adams* (New York: Simon & Schuster, 2001), 97.

29. Ibid., 373-4.

30. Ibid., 418.

31. Matthew 5:15.

32. Later caught by the Gestapo, Helmuth was charged with conspiracy to commit high treason and sentenced to death. He was the youngest person to be executed by the Nazis.

33. 2 Kings 6:15-17.

34. Sun Tzu, *The Art of War*, 44.

35. Allan H. Gilbert, ed., *Machiavelli: The Chief Works and Others, vol. 2* (Duke University Press, 1965), 697.

36. Frank Mehring, *Karl Marx: The Story of His Life* (London: George Allen & Unwin Ltd, 1936), 127.

37. David Brooks, "The Nuclear Family Was a Mistake," *The Atlantic*, March 2020, https://www.theatlantic.com/magazine/archive/2020/03/the-nuclear-family-was-a-mistake/605536/.

38. "Martin Niemöller: 'First They Came For…'," Holocaust Encyclopedia, accessed August 14, 2022, https://encyclopedia.ushmm.org/content/en/article/martin-niemoeller-first-they-came-for-the-socialists.

39. Ibid.

40. See "Political Polarization in the American Public," Pew Research Center, June 12, 2014, https://www.pewresearch.org/politics/2014/06/12/political-polarization-in-the-american-public/.

CONCLUSION

1. For documented detail on these events, see Victor Sebestyen, *Twelve Days: The Story of the 1956 Hungarian Revolution* (New York: Vintage Books, 2007).

2. James Michener, *The Bridge at Andau* (New York: Dial Press, 2015), 146.

3. Ibid.

4. Ibid.

5. Ibid., 150.

6. Ibid., 149.

7. Ibid.

8. Ibid.

9. Novak, *The Spirit of Democratic Capitalism*, 165.

10. "Putin Aims to Shape a New Generation of Supporters, Through Schools," The New York Times, July 16, 2022, https://www.nytimes.com/2022/07/16/world/europe/russia-putin-schools-propaganda-indoctrination.html.

11. Ibid.

THE AUTHOR

Connor Boyack is the founder and president of Libertas Institute, a free-market think tank in Utah. In that capacity, he has spearheaded a number of successful policy reforms in areas such as education, civil liberties, government transparency, business deregulation, medical freedom, and more. Several of these legal changes were the first of their kind in the country, and Libertas Institute has received numerous awards for its innovative work.

A public speaker and author of over three dozen books, Connor is best known for the *Tuttle Twins* books, a children's series introducing young readers to economic, political, and civic principles. Over four million copies have been sold in a dozen different languages. He is also an executive producer for the Tuttle Twins animated cartoon series based on the books.

Connor lives near Salt Lake City, Utah, with his wife and two homeschooled children.

Learn more at ConnorBoyack.com